The Official
Tortoise Trust Guide

to

Tortoises & Turtles

their care & maintenance in captivity

By

A. C. Highfield

Second Edition

London – England

D1127304

Second Edition, first impression 1994

ISBN 1 873943 01 6

Published by
Carapace Press
c/o The Tortoise Trust
BM Tortoise
London
WC1N 3XX
England
Tel/Fax 0267-211578

Distributed in USA by
Serpent's Tale
464 Second Street
Excelsior, MN 55331
USA
Fax 612-470-5013

Printed & bound by Gomer Press, Llandysul, Dyfed, Wales, SA44 4BQ

INTRODUCTION

The Tortoise Trust was conceived in the `dark days' of the bulk trade, when box-loads of sad tortoises could be seen each spring in the windows of a hundred dingy pet shops. Most of those animals (which live 50 or more years in the wild) would be dead within 12 months of becoming a pet, although a few of these early imports do still survive. Tortoises at that time were often regarded like many people today regard their cars - replaced every year by a `new model'.

It has always seemed strange to me that an animal about which zoologists, biologists and paleontologists actually know so little could, by the simple expedient of removing it from its natural habitat, be suddenly transformed into a common tortoise which could be purchased for a few pennies and was not worthy of 'serious' attention. If it died, so what? You could always buy another one next year. After all, it was just a tortoise and there were plenty more where that came from.

The result was that for many years literally hundreds of thousands of tortoises were collected annually for sale as `disposable' pets. Hardly anyone knew - or cared - what the effects of this would be on wild populations and so what has been described as the great `tortoise drain' continued.

Things are, however, changing - slowly. The bulk trade in most species has ended at last and those people who do keep tortoises on the whole now treat them much more seriously and with greater care and respect than ever before. Many enthusiasts are also increasingly involving themselves in conservation efforts, trying to give something back to tortoises instead of merely taking from them.

It is not only land tortoises which have suffered as a result of large-scale trade collecting of course, aquatic turtles have also been exploited in vast numbers. Unlike the land tortoise trade however, the turtle business is still thriving and millions are sold each year. The majority are just as unlikely to survive in the long-term as their terrestrial relatives in earlier years.

By caring properly for those tortoises which are already in captivity, by campaigning vigorously for the protection and preservation of those remaining in the wild, and by learning and eventually passing on our knowledge of and concern for tortoises to others, at last we can begin to repay the tremendous debt we owe these most gentle and mysterious creatures.

This is a very practical book. It contains a lot of the special knowledge gained over the years by those of us who have been extraordinarily privileged to be able to work with tortoises on an everyday basis at the Tortoise Trust's sanctuary and at the Tortoise Hospital. We have often stayed up all night with acutely sick tortoises, we have been devastated sometimes when all our efforts have failed, and there have been joyous moments too when tiny heads have peered out of their eggs for the first time or a patient made a `miracle' recovery against all the odds. It has often been hard and demanding work, but I know that given the chance we would each do it all over again and we wouldn't change a thing.

I hope you like it. And even more, I hope your tortoises like it too. *Because this book is for them.*

Patient at the Tortoise Trust sanctuary

BASIC PRACTICAL CARE

Before moving on to describe in detail the requirements of captive tortoises and turtles, it is worth taking a short time out to cover a few very basic facts which are nonetheless frequently the cause of a great deal of misunderstanding and confusion. We are often asked about these particular points by worried or curious owners, and there is no doubt that even people who might have kept tortoises for many years are often misinformed on these matters. Unfortunately, tortoise keeping is littered with a veritable mythology of half-truths and misconstrued facts. Even more unfortunately it is a sad fact that many of the books on tortoises and turtles likely to be consulted by pet owners add to rather than diminish that confusion. For a change, you can rely completely upon the accuracy of the information which follows here.

HOW DO YOU TELL THE AGE OF A TORTOISE?

It is often said that it is possible to tell the age of a tortoise by counting the growth rings which are generally visible on each scute; in fact, this is not entirely true and the method is somewhat unreliable to say the least.

There are several reasons for this.

Firstly, in extremely aged tortoises the growth rings are rarely visible at all, having long ago been abraded or worn off. Secondly, tortoises do not always deposit a single growth ring for every year of age but may lay down several. Even in the wild I have seen hatchlings of no more than 2 years of age which clearly had six or even seven growth rings visible. Some of our own captive-bred hatchlings which are less than 6 months old already have 2 very clear growth rings. Counting growth rings (even if it is possible) is not therefore likely to lead to very accurate results. It is also worth noting that not all species deposit clearly visible growth rings in the first place - the Redfoot tortoise (*Chelonoidis carbonaria*) is one of these.

Another misleading myth insists that the larger a tortoise is the older it is. Once again, this is completely untrue. Size is actually determined by genetics and some species are naturally very much larger or smaller than others. Obvious examples include Seychelles and Galapagos giant tortoises at the larger extreme and little Egyptian tortoises or Madagascan Spider tortoises at the other. Even within what are generally regarded as Mediterranean species there is quite a size range. For example, in Algeria there is an unusually large species of localised distribution which attains an average size of 280mm long in the case of females and 225mm long in the case of males. In neighbouring Tunisia, however, the little coastal tortoises (*Furculachelys nabeulensis*) measure no more than 150mm long if they are female whilst most males measure less than 130mm. Before this was understood, all of the Tunisian tortoises were assumed to be juvenile specimens by the few herpetologists who had bothered to study them!

Therefore, in order to establish the age of a tortoise with reasonable accuracy it is necessary to:

- assess the degree of carapace wear.

- compare this with average growth data for the same species.

This method has the advantage that it can be used successfully with all species, including those which do not normally exhibit identifiable growth rings.

If a tortoise is correctly identified as to species and is very close to the absolute maximum size reached by adults of that species it would generally be at least 20 years of age. If in addition it features a considerable amount of carapace wear then it is almost certainly very much older. By the time most tortoises reach 75-80 years of age they are looking fairly worn and battered. Extremely aged tortoises (90-100 years plus) are invariably very eroded and usually show signs of having lost the outermost layer of the scutes.

This results in certain colour changes which are quite characteristic.

Determining the age of a tortoise with reasonable accuracy has an important role in captive breeding; trying to breed from elderly females can have fatal consequences and should be avoided.

HOW LONG DO TORTOISES & TURTLES LIVE?

The absolute maximum natural life-span of a tortoise is not entirely certain, but I do know of several confirmed instances where tortoises have survived for over 70 years in captivity, and many more where they have survived for 50 years. These tortoises were by no means hatchlings when originally obtained so their actual ages are probably in the region of 90 to 100 years. The oldest Mediterranean tortoise I have personally encountered had an estimated age of 130 years. Surprisingly, even some small species such as American Box turtles are known to be capable of living to over 100 years of age and it seems likely that some very large species such as Seychelles and Galapagos giants may live over 200 years.

IS IT MALE OR FEMALE?

There are a number of external signs or characteristics, which can be used to determine the sex of tortoises and turtles. However, these signs do vary quite a lot between individual species and so without a considerable amount of experience on behalf of the observer can be quite difficult to interpret. Generally speaking however, the following characteristics provide a pretty reliable indication:

Plastron

If the plastron is curved or depressed inwards then this is a good indication that the tortoise is a male. The greatest degree of plastral concavity is seen in some tropical tortoises such as the Redfoot tortoise (*Chelonoidis carbonaria*) but the same character occurs to a lesser extent in the males of most species. Where the plastron is entirely flat this usually indicates that the tortoise is a female.

Once again however there are some exceptions, and no single character should be considered diagnostic by itself. In Box turtles males do have a slightly depressed plastron and thicker tail, but the difference is very slight. If you are unused to comparing them it is easy to make a mistake.

Tail length

Above: *Male tortoises have much longer tails than females.*

Below: *Females have short, stubby tails.*

Almost without exception, male tortoises have much longer tails than females. This is particularly clear in the case of Hermann's tortoises (*Testudo hermanni*) but is also true of just about every other species. As a very general rule, if the tail is long enough to be carried tucked up and sideways when the tortoise walks along it is a male; if it is short and stubby then in all probability it is a female. There are a few exceptions to this and some tortoises can be extremely difficult to sex accurately - American Box turtles (*Terrapene* species) and Chaco tortoises (*Chelonoidis chilensis*) are particularly problematic in that visible external differences between males and females are not only slight but are also subject to considerable variability.

Supracaudal scute

The supracaudal scute is located immediately above the tail and is the last in the series of vertebral scutes. In some species the supracaudal scute of adult males is bulbous and incurved whereas in females of the species it is relatively flat. This is not true of all species, but this character is certainly present in many and where present is a fairly reliable indicator of sex.

Carapace profile

In many species females have a higher `dome' to their shells than males. Females also tend to be wider at the mid-line than males. Nowhere is this observed to better effect than in the case of Redfoot tortoises.

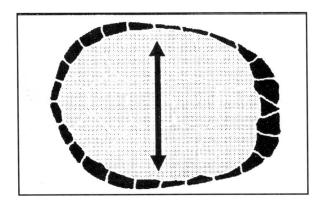

Above: Female tortoises tend to be broader at the midline than males.

Size

In most species of tortoise females attain larger maximum adult dimensions than males. This difference and the other differences mentioned above are known to zoologists as dimorphic characters. The main exception to the general rule that male tortoises tend to be smaller than females is to be found on the Galapagos islands where for some evolutionary reason or another the males are considerably larger than the females - a similar thing is also seen in the African Spurred tortoise (*Geochelone sulcata*) and in the South African Angulate tortoise (*Chersina angulata*). It is important to remember that dimorphic characters can only be compared within the same species. If two entirely different species are compared the results will be totally misleading.

Other ways to tell

These characters are often specific, that is, they are of use only within the confines of a single species or genus. As there are over 40 currently recognised species of land tortoise alone, the number of specific dimorphic characters is therefore very large (although they are by no means unique in every case). For a good example of such a character we have only to look closely at a pair of Three-toed American Box turtles (*Terrapene carolina triunguis*). Although externally very similar, on close examination it will be noted that most males have reddish-orange eyes whilst most females have deep brown eyes. With many aquatic turtles the males are not only smaller, but also have much longer claws or `fingers' on the front legs; getting to know the significance of these various specific characters is essential if you hope to breed tortoises or turtles with any degree of success.

TORTOISE, TURTLE OR TERRAPIN?

In the United States it is customary to call all members of the shield reptile group `turtles' whether they live on the land or in the water. In Britain and most of Europe a slightly different terminology is preferred in which tortoises are exclusively or mainly land dwellers, turtles are sea-going or marine dwellers and terrapins are freshwater aquatic testudines. In respect of native American species such as Box and Wood turtles however, it has generally become accepted that these should be known colloquially as `turtles' even though they are mainly terrestrial in habit.

Biologically, true tortoises cannot swim (or can do so only with the greatest difficulty and then only for a short time), whilst turtles and terrapins are excellent swimmers. There are other biological differences involving the carapace, foot structure and respiration in particular.

On a practical note, be sure to securely fence all ponds in areas where terrestrial tortoises have access. Each summer without fail we receive several distressing reports of tortoises drowning by accident after they have fallen into unprotected garden ponds. *Consult the first aid section for more advice on what to do if you are confronted with an apparently drowned tortoise.*

WHAT IS THE IDEAL DIET FOR A TORTOISE OR TURTLE?

We probably receive more questions on this topic than on all of the others put together as the `correct'

4

diet for captive tortoises and turtles has long been a somewhat confused and often contentious issue; much of the advice in circulation is contradictory and (usually) extremely outdated. *A lot of it is also just plain wrong.*

Clearly, the `ideal' diet for any pet tortoise or turtle would be exactly the same as it experiences in the wild. For obvious reasons, this is not usually possible but it does eliminate some of the more bizarre items which have been suggested from time to time as suitable. When anything is suggested as a suitable food to feed your pet tortoise, it's a good idea to ask the following question:

• Would this particular species eat this (or something very like it) in the wild?

If the answer is `No', then it is probably *not* a good idea to include that item in the diet. At least not regularly.

Tortoises and turtles do not normally suffer from dietary deficiencies or dietary excesses in their wild state. They eat a very varied range of suitable foodstuffs and do very well indeed on them. It follows that the more varied diet you can offer a captive tortoise or turtle the better, but only things which match the dietary profile of the animal in the wild. In the case of true land tortoises that really means green weeds, leaf vegetables and some fruits. Not all vegetable foods are totally safe if provided in excess however; some high fat, high phosphate items such as avocado, or bananas, are definitely not a good idea as habitual foodstuffs. They may be used occasionally, but too frequent usage may cause problems. Beanshoots for example are very strongly calcium to phosphorus (Ca:P) deficient and can definitely cause problems (especially with hatchlings). *These too are best avoided.*

In captivity, most experienced keepers consider that it is very important to provide a mineral-vitamin supplement with the basic diet as this supplies many of the trace elements often missing in `prepared' food as opposed to what a tortoise or turtle obtains in the wild, where it consumes grit and trace elements in the form of earth and mud with its food. Products are available from specialist suppliers and veterinary surgeons which contain a wide range of these trace elements plus a useful quantity of vitamins, especially vitamin-A and the `sunshine vitamin' D3 which is essential to healthy bone growth. Grated cuttlefish also helps, but even better is a non-phosphate calcium source such as calcium carbonate or calcium lactate. Certain vegetables can be quite rich in phosphates, and the addition of raw calcium to

the diet helps to counterbalance this. In the case of meat eating turtles, raw calcium supplementation is even more critical.

Feeding land tortoises

In the wild, tortoises typically consume from 4 to 6 parts calcium (Ca) to 1 part phosphorus (P) and the maintenance of this balance (which is known as the Ca:P ratio) is vitally important to the overall well-being and safe growth of your tortoise. A reversed or retarded Ca:P ratio, where the level of calcium falls below about 1.2:1 is extremely dangerous. It causes

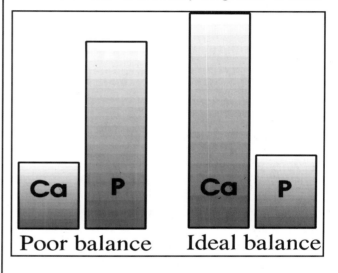

This graph shows the relationship of calcium to phosphorus in a good and bad captive diet. Where the intake of calcium is less than adequate, severe bone deformities will occur.

several serious formative and growth disorders including a condition where the bones are unable to obtain enough calcium to grow properly; they become malformed, porous and soft. This is sometimes seen in young tortoises which have been subject to an incorrect diet and in its worst form is called soft-shell disease. The cause is a diet rich in phosphates and poor in calcium. The most acute cases of all are generally seen in tortoises which have been starved of calcium and its associated metabolising vitamin (D3) but which have been fed on high protein items such as dog food or beanshoots which are invariably strongly Ca:P negative.

Another condition is seen in egg laying female tortoises where the eggs are so thin-walled that they fracture during laying. Peritonitis often results.

Suggested diet for Mediterranean tortoises

❑ Dandelion
❑ Vetches
❑ Some 'commercial' green vegetables
❑ Fresh clean grass
❑ Small quantity of fruit (irregularly only)
❑ Tomato (small quantity)
❑ Cucumber or squash (small quantity)
❑ As much natural graze and browsing as possible

The calcium deficiency problems listed above can be entirely prevented by supplying a carefully balanced natural diet combined with the careful use of appropriate supplements. The suggested diet however also contains two other basic ingredients essential to all tortoises.

Dietary fibre

Fibre is required to help the tortoise's digestion. Without an adequate dietary fibre intake tortoises tend to suffer from diarrhoea and loose motions. Frequently, these problems can be cured simply by increasing the amount of coarse, fibrous vegetable matter provided in the food. Grass is probably the most natural source, and most tortoises enjoy it. Very coarse cabbage and cauliflower is also useful in this respect.

Water

Water is very important to all tortoises. If dehydration occurs, then kidney problems very rapidly follow. You can help maintain adequate hydration by adopting three simple methods:

• Include at least some high-water content fruits in every meal. Good examples include tomato, melon, cucumber and plums etc. (but be careful about including too many sugar-rich items in the diet as these can cause problems of their own).

• Always provide a shallow drinking dish; ideally, this should be large enough for the entire tortoise to climb into, and about 20mm deep for an average sized animal. Change the water every day. Encourage all tortoises to take a regular `bath' and have a drink.

• Do not bring tortoises inside at the first sign of rain - rain encourages tortoises to both drink and urinate; this is good for the kidneys and in any case, most tortoises enjoy a warm, summery shower!

Protein

It is important at the outset to dispense with the dangerous myth that the higher the protein content of a diet, the better `quality' that diet is. Certainly in the case of tortoises which have evolved over millions of years to survive on a very low protein diet an excessively high level of dietary protein is not just detrimental to health - it is positively lethal.

In terms of a tortoises natural diet, grass is actually a fairly rich source of protein - items such as peas, beans or (worse still) meat-based cat and dog foods are highly damaging to tortoises.

High protein foods result in a dangerous increase in blood urea levels, *this causes renal stress and can lead to complete kidney failure.* It is also a contributory factor in a very nasty condition known as articular gout where concentrated uric acid deposits infiltrate the joints of the limbs.

Generally speaking, the higher the protein level of a particular foodstuff the worse its Ca:P ratio is. Meat, for example, may be 1:40 against. We have already noted that tortoises actually need a positive ratio of approximately 5:1 or greater. Peas and beans are similarly strongly calcium:phosphate negative.

Most high protein foods are also rich in fats; tinned cat and dog foods are by far the worst in this respect and can contain up to 25% saturated fat and oil. Most land tortoises, being natural herbivores, are designed to exist quite happily on a diet containing nil saturated fat and only very low levels of vegetable fat. If placed on fat rich diets liver problems are sure to follow. Such tortoises also tend to be grossly overweight. In addition, a high fat diet actually reduces the animal's ability to absorb what calcium is present in the diet - *so it is even more damaging than might be evident at first.* There is no scientific evidence which supports the use of unnatural food items. All recommendations to employ such foodstuffs (*e.g.* dog or cat food to herbivores) are based upon a basic misunderstanding of tortoise biology, evolution and natural behaviour patterns. The advice to include tinned cat or dog food in the diet of Mediterranean tortoises is often seen; my own reaction is to wonder how many of the people issuing such inaccurate and dangerous advice have any first-hand knowledge of these animals in the wild? Having studied tortoises on both sides of the Mediterranean and in their natural habitat for some years, it is very evident to me that animal protein does not form any regular component of their diet. One study concluded that wild *Testudo graeca* regularly consumed over 150 different plant species as part of their regular diet - but no evidence of carnivorous intake was found. *They don't need meat in the wild, and they don't need it in captivity either.* The Tortoise Trust raises Mediterranean tortoise hatchlings to adulthood on 100% vegetable diets; these animals are totally healthy, grow at rates comparable to wild tortoises and have perfectly formed undistorted carapaces. They should be compared to the lumpy shelled and weak, but grotesquely overgrown specimens raised on cat or dog food. Most of these die before reaching adulthood from kidney and liver disease induced by poor dietary management. There are numerous reasons to avoid feeding animal proteins to biological herbivores - the catastrophic effects of doing so are well established and are measurable - and absolutely no benefits. Despite what you might read or hear to the contrary, your tortoise will be infinitely better off without it.

Feeding aquatic turtles

The diet of most terrapins and turtles is, by contrast to land tortoises, heavily dependent upon animal protein. Most aquatic and semi-aquatic turtles and terrapins are predators and catch a wide range of fish, snails and similar small creatures. These provide not only protein but also calcium in balanced amounts (whole animals are eaten - bones included - not just the fleshy parts). In captivity it is essential not to make the all-too-common mistake of feeding only the `best' meat minus the calcium containing bones! Large bone splinters can, however, prove to be a danger in their own right if swallowed whole so many keepers prefer to provide calcium in a safer form (usually as a proprietary supplement).

Most terrapins and turtles are actually **omnivorous** rather than exclusively carnivorous, consuming both animal prey *and* plant material in the wild. This pattern should be encouraged in captivity. Some are definitely more carnivorous than others, but even my voracious Common Snapping turtle (*Chelydra serpentina*) has been known to take plants in preference to its more usual meaty fare on rare occasions. In all cases, however, it is certainly not adequate to feed only on commercial 'turtle flakes' which are often of very poor nutritional value and severely lacking in dietary fibre, vitamins and minerals. Nor should whitebait or similar fish form the staple diet, as these are excessively rich in oil and can result in steatitis or fatty infiltration of the liver. Diets containing excessive quantities of fish can also result in induced vitamin-B deficiencies due to the presence in fish of an enzyme called thiaminase, which interferes with the take up of B-group vitamins.

The main thing to avoid with diets for any captive turtle is over-reliance upon one single item; this is a very easy mistake to make, but a balanced and varied diet is infinitely superior. Provide as wide a range of the following food items as you possibly can. It is also worth noting that the sex of certain turtles affects their preferred diet; for example, female Common Map Turtles (*Graptemys geographica*) have a much wider mouth than males and therefore take larger prey. Whereas the females of this species feed predominantly upon large snails and other molluscs, the males prey mainly upon aquatic insects and smaller snails.

Suggested terrapin/turtle diet

- ❑ Plant leaf material
- ❑ Fruit
- ❑ Canned dog food (low lat varieties preferred)
- ❑ Raw (whole) fish
- ❑ Rehydrated dried cat, dog or trout pellets
- ❑ Fresh meat
- ❑ Earthworms
- ❑ Snails and molluscs
- ❑ Small dead rodents such as mice

Where food is to be rehydrated, as with the dried cat or dog pellets available in pet stores, rehydrate using water plus a soluble vitamin additive. This is a highly successful way of ensuring that your turtle will obtain all of the essential vitamins and trace elements it requires.

To avoid contaminating your turtles with *Salmonella* organisms, it is wise not to feed raw chicken or pork - these frequently harbour the organism and if eaten by the turtle the disease will be passed on. *Diets rich in meats are invariably also high in phosphates and low in calcium.* This can cause serious problems for terrapins who need high levels of calcium for healthy bone and carapace development. Note that in the wild most aquatic testudines feed regularly upon snails and similar creatures which have a calcium-rich shell. In captivity, this source is rarely available and therefore additional calcium supplementation is absolutely essential. Calcium tablets can be successfully hidden in meats, and all foods heavily dusted with a general high ratio calcium-mineral supplement such as Nutrobal®. Provision of a cuttlefish bone which can be gnawed if required is also recommended.

Finally on the topic of feeding, it is definitely the case in my experience that over-rather than underfeeding tends to be the main problem in many captive situations; in the long term this can prove just as damaging as underfeeding. Not only must the quality of the diet be maintained within safe limits, but the quantity too. This applies equally to land tortoises and aquatic turtles; in the latter case if you overfeed you will not only get fatty, obese and lethargic turtles but you will also very quickly experience serious tank hygiene problems - and an almost certain outcome of that will be a dramatic increase in the incidence of infectious disease. In most cases, feeding 3 times per week will be quite adequate. *Daily feeding is hardly ever required with aquatic testudines.*

Feeding Box & Wood turtles

These North American semi-aquatic turtles are omnivorous in their feeding habits. In the wild, they consume slugs, snails, earthworms and similar small prey as well as fallen fruits, mushrooms and some green leaf material. Juvenile Box turtles are often almost exclusively carnivorous, their diet broadening out to include more vegetable matter with increasing age.

Suggested diet for Box & Wood turtles

- ❑ Slugs
- ❑ Earthworms
- ❑ Snails
- ❑ Fruit
- ❑ Green leaf vegetables
- ❑ Mushrooms
- ❑ Small quantity (low fat) dog food

As with all tortoises and turtles, great care must be taken to ensure a varied diet adequate in all essential trace elements. Regular supplementation of the diet with a vitamin-mineral powder is therefore recommended.

Feeding tropical tortoises

The term 'tropical tortoise' covers a very diverse range of animals, from even more varied habitats. From tortoises which live in semi-arid desert such as *Geochelone sulcata* (African Spurred tortoise), to tortoises of the grassy savannahs such as *Geochelone pardalis* (Leopard tortoise), through rain-forest animals such as *Geochelone denticulata* (Yellow-

foot tortoise) and some (not all) members of the *Kinixys* (Hinge-back) group.

From the above it will be clear that no single diet can be recommended as suitable for such a wide range of

Above: *Geochelone carbonaria, the tropical Redfoot tortoise. It prefers an omnivorous diet.*

tortoises with such different preferences and requirements. However, it is possible to make a few general recommendations based upon our own and our members' experience of keeping all of the above mentioned species. Firstly, most tropical species' diets can be broadly categorised as either;

Entirely herbivorous
or
Omnivorous

There are no *entirely* carnivorous land tortoises. From this, it follows that for practical purposes, all tropical tortoise diets can be accommodated by combining elements from the suggestions given above designed either for herbivorous land tortoises such as *T. graeca* or *T. hermanni* or for semi-carnivorous aquatic testudines such as terrapins or Box turtles. The problem for keepers is to know which diet suits which particular tortoise. The following guide-lines provide a useful starting point based upon our personal experience:

Leopard tortoises, African Spurred tortoises and Chaco tortoises

These are almost exclusively herbivorous. Provide diet as for *Testudo* species. Also note that these tortoises enjoy grazing on grass and that the fibre content of this seems to be important in maintaining a healthy digestion.

Above: Geochelone sulcata: African Spurred tortoise, a very large herbivorous species. Like many such tortoises, a high fibre diet is critical.

Red-foot and Yellow-foot tortoises; Bell's, Eroded & Home's Hinge-back tortoises

These tortoises are basically omnivorous or a greater or lesser extent. Precise tastes vary. Include some low-fat animal protein in the diet. Protein-deficiency has been noted in some Red-foot and Yellow-foot tortoises raised on *entirely* herbivorous diets (see 'The Sick Tortoise or Turtle'). We recommend re-hydrating dried cat foots with additional minerals and vitamins as for terrapins. Provide one meal per week containing animal protein. We give about 50g of moist cat food to a fully grown Red-foot tortoise on a weekly basis. The same frequency seems to suit Hinge-backs, but here 10-20g is more appropriate (depending upon size). It is also important to note that these tortoises, if allowed access to a damp, moist garden or well vegetated tropical house will find slugs and snails for themselves. This is both psychologically and gastronomically stimulating for them in addition to helping out with their owners' garden pest control efforts! Needless to say, never use slug pellets or other toxic chemicals in any garden where tortoises (of any sort) are kept.

Feeding questions & answers

We are very often asked for specific advice on feeding tortoises and turtles, and many times we find ourselves answering the same questions several times a week - we have therefore summarised some of the most frequently asked questions below together with our responses.

Will bonemeal or ground cuttlefish sprinkled on the food prevent `softshell' problems?

As explained previously, the important point to bear in mind is not just the net quantity of calcium provided, but its *ratio* to phosphorus. Unfortunately any bone-based supplement will also contain its own phosphorus (frequently at quite a high concentration), therefore, it will not be as effective in balancing any residual calcium deficiency in the main diet as a non-phosphate source. The use of a specially formulated calcium balancer such as Nutrobal , or simple raw calcium additive such as calcium carbonate, is infinitely better. The rate at which tortoises absorb calcium is very inefficient; often only 20% to 30% of ingested calcium is actually absorbed. The rate of absorption also depends upon other factors such as the availability of vitamin D3. For that reason, and especially in critical situations (*e.g* in hatchlings or carnivorous turtles where deficiencies occur very readily) we recommend using a combined vitamin-mineral supplement with a high calcium-low phosphorus content.

I have read a lot about the dangers of underweight tortoises, but is it possible for them to become overweight?

Definitely. We see a large number of overweight animals. A seriously overweight tortoise or turtle is at considerable risk. One of the first functions to suffer is the liver, which can degenerate rapidly as a result of excess fat. In most cases obesity in tortoises and turtles can be traced directly to an incorrect diet. Items such as cheese, egg or other high fat foods are totally inappropriate and should never be given.

My tortoise is a very fussy eater, and will only take a very limited range of foods. Also, it refuses to

touch anything if I apply a vitamin supplement to it. Is there anything I can do to overcome this behaviour?

In these circumstances, we find that if allowed to become sufficiently hungry even the fussiest of tortoises will eventually take whatever is offered. This can take a while however. If the existing diet is inadequate or incorrect (e.g the tortoise has become addicted to cat or dog food), then it is essential that the dietary regime is rectified as soon as possible and this may well involve removing the offending items from the diet immediately. As a result, the tortoise may well refuse to take any alternatives offered. Provided that the tortoise is a good weight, and is not allowed to become dehydrated, then a few days or even weeks of not feeding are unlikely to do any harm. It must, however, be monitored carefully during the transition phase.

My tortoise often eats stones, and I would like to know what purpose this behaviour serves and wonder if it presents any danger?

There are two main possibilities. Firstly, if your tortoise is eating white stones, this can indicate a desire for additional calcium (in Africa, Leopard tortoises are often seen gnawing on bleached skeletons for just this reason). Another possibility is that the tortoise is seeking more roughage, and the provision of extra fibre in the diet can sometimes eliminate stone-eating. However, there is good evidence that even under `ideal' natural conditions tortoises - and turtles - do sometimes consume stones, dirt and grit. These may play some role in digestion, may provide an additional source of mineral trace-elements, or there may be another as yet unknown motivation for the behaviour. Either way, although there may be a slight theoretical risk, the chances of any real harm being sustained as a result must be regarded as very remote.

I am very concerned that my tortoise rarely (if ever) drinks. Is this normal?

It very much depends. If your base-line diet is very rich in fluid (*e.g* tomatoes, cucumber etc.) then quite possibly the tortoise is getting all it needs from that. However, most tortoises do enjoy a drink and if water is offered in the right way will take the opportunity. There are three good ways to encourage drinking;

you can place the entire tortoise in a shallow bowl of water filled so that it just reaches the tortoise's lower jaw - most will drink if water is offered in this way; you can also gently spray the tortoise with a hose-pipe on a hot summer's day - again, this frequently encourages them to take a drink. Finally, leave the tortoise out in the rain for a while. This will not do any harm at all (it rains in the wild!) and often you will see their heads go down to a shallow puddle. Incidentally, tortoises very frequently urinate simultaneously with drinking. This is a highly developed strategy designed to conserve as much vital fluid within the body as possible until it can definitely be replaced. Concurrent drinking and urination occurs in many species, but is particularly common in those species which experience hot dry seasons where water is periodically scarce. In heavy rainfalls some species become very active - observe *T. hermanni* or *G. elegans* (the Indian Star tortoise) for example. These tortoises greatly enjoy the rain, and will raise up on their hind legs to urinate whilst `browsing' the raindrops from wet grass at the front! This encourages healthy kidney activity and prevents dehydration.

My tortoise lives in a large garden, and I rarely provide any additional food other than the plants it grazes on naturally. Is there any danger of under-feeding ?

In a sufficiently large and suitably planted area a tortoise can indeed not only survive, but thrive, under these conditions. However, it is vitally important to keep a constant watch on the animal's weight and to make regular visual checks to ensure that it is feeding normally. Only the large and thickly planted gardens tend to be suitable for this method of maintenance.

I have a pair of Red-eared terrapins in an indoor tank, but they frequently leave a lot of the food I provide uneaten. This makes the tank smelly and unpleasant. Is there a better way to feed them?

This is a very typical case of over-feeding. Cut down drastically on the quantity and frequency of feeds. General tank hygiene will also be improved by installing a good power filter and avoiding greasy, oily foods.

My Box turtles live outdoors for

most of the year. How can I ensure that they obtain a natural-type diet?

In most cases, some additional feeding is recommended for these turtles, but you can often increase the quantity of natural food which is available by placing some flat roof tiles on the ground within their enclosure and watering these regularly. Large numbers of earth worms, crickets, slugs and beetles will be attracted which will provide a valuable source of natural prey.

Above: *American Box turtle*

North American Wood Turtle Clemmys insculpta - now becoming rarer in the wild

Photo courtesy of Ashley Woods

CONSERVATION ISSUES

Above

Stuffed sea turtles, elephant feet and skins from endangered mammals and reptiles constitute a massive illegal trade and pose a critical threat to many species. This trade is also cruel and barbaric in the extreme. Be aware of the problem and educate fellow travellers when on vacation abroad.

Right

Musical instruments made from the carapaces of *Testudo graeca* on sale in Morocco. These tortoises were killed just to make these grisly 'souvenirs'. Avoid at all costs and ask others to do the same.

GENERAL CARE & MAINTENANCE

In the correct captive environment most tortoises and turtles do not require a great deal of human intervention. However, they do require careful checking and monitoring. If the environment is anything less than ideal (and it is by no means easy to set up a `perfect' environment for such climatically and environmentally sensitive animals) then they will require far more direct attention and intervention. In the wild, chelonians have access to a wide range of natural foodstuffs and without exception they live in an environment which is climatically perfectly suited to their biological needs. The particular combination of natural factors within which a species evolved and lives naturally includes such variables as climate, vegetation, photo-period (*e.g* daylength) and soil texture; this is collectively known to zoologists as the `biotype'.

In captivity both food availability and climate are

Typical forest habitat of Testudo graeca graeca in North Africa.

often very different to those experienced under natural circumstances . Hence, keepers have to invest a great deal of time and energy in an effort to compensate for some of these less-than-ideal circumstances and to duplicate the naturally occurring biotype as closely as possible.

It is important in this respect not to make the mistake of assuming that a good captive environment must look exactly like the natural habitat - what looks attractive and `natural' to humans may in fact not offer the best combination of environmental suitability or safety. Too much emphasis is all too often placed on how natural an enclosure looks, and not enough on how well a safe and clean environment can be maintained.

Although almost every individual species has at least some very specific habitat, dietary or climatic requirements almost all tortoises and turtles can be usefully placed into one or other of a relatively small number of groups for practical captive maintenance purposes. Briefly, these can be summarised as follows.

GROUP 1

Exclusively land dwelling temperate tortoises

One common factor linking these tortoises is that they normally experience a winter hibernation. Another common factor is that they are naturally almost exclusively herbivorous and do not require any meat products in their diet. Typical temperature requirements include daytime temperatures in the order of 15°-30°C which can fall to 10°-12°C overnight. Tortoises from temperate zones experience very variable weather conditions in the wild, with quite poor weather on occasions - especially at the beginning and end of the season. This is perfectly natural, and provided the overall conditions under which they are to be maintained are satisfactory (especially during the all-important summer period) a bit of cold or wet weather does them no harm whatsoever. Prolonged cold or wet periods however *can* pose problems. At such times, an artificial (indoor or greenhouse) environment should be considered.

GROUP 2

Exclusively land dwelling tropical tortoises

This group consists of all truly tropical zone tortoises from such diverse locations as South America, Asia and central and southern Africa. The major difference from temperate species, such as those from the Mediterranean region, is that they do not hibernate in the winter. In addition, most of these tortoises require generally fairly constant temperatures and relatively high humidity. Typical temperature requirements are for 23°-29°C both day and night with moderate to very high humidity depending on the species. Some fairly typical tropical zone dwellers include Redfoot tortoises (*C. carbonaria*) and Hinge-back tortoises (*Kinixys* species). Most of these tortoises are largely herbivorous, but some do consume small quantities of animal protein on occasions, *e.g* in the form of slugs or snails. Even within a single genus, precise care requirements can differ considerably. For example, if we look at the Hingeback tortoises, clear differences emerge between the three most commonly encountered species:

Bell's Hinged tortoise (*Kinixys belliana*)

This is the most widely distributed of the Kinixys species, and occurs from West Africa and Senegal to Natal in South Africa and extending into Madagascar. This tortoise is by far the most environmentally tolerant of the entire Kinixys group, and is found in a variety of habitats ranging from the very humid to the relatively arid. There is some evidence that in very dry conditions this tortoise aestivates underground to await the rains, at the onset of which it becomes very active and breeding activity occurs. Aestivation - or 'summer retreat' - must not be confused with hibernation, which is biologically a very different condition. Unlike Mediterranean tortoises, Bell's Hinged tortoise is omnivorous, and feeds on slugs, giant land snails, worms, fungi, fallen fruits and leaves. Juveniles are generally more carnivorous than adults. In captivity, this tortoise is partial to tomatoes, banana and re-hydrated dried cat food (which should be given in moderation) but 'live' prey should also be offered.

Eroded Hinge-back tortoise (*Kinixys erosa*)

This tortoise has been described as looking very much like an up-turned leaf. It is certainly a very distinctive animal. It occurs in Uganda and the Congo northwest to the Gambia. There are further records from Ghana, the Ivory Coast and the Cameroon. It is a very secretive and environmentally delicate creature, whose natural habitat centres mainly upon shady river banks, marshes and the edges of rain forest. It is the largest of the Hinge-back species, and can measure up to 300mm long. In captivity, it requires very careful maintenance and a consistently high level of humidity. A bathing area should be provided at all times. If humidity is inadequate it will suffer immediate eye, nose and ear problems. Its dietary requirements are as for Bell's Hinge-back tortoise, but *K. erosa* is much more likely to feed at dawn or dusk. It tends to avoid bright daylight, even when feeding or mating.

Kinixys homeana

Homes Hinged tortoise (*Kinixys homeana*)

Also originating in West Africa, superficially this tortoise is very similar to the Eroded Hinge-back described above. It is however distinguished on close examination by having a darker coloured head, a more acute angular rear carapace profile, and is considerably smaller than its near relative whose habitat and dietary preferences it shares.

The message is clear. *Don't generalise.* Learn all you can about the tortoises you keep and adjust their diet and environment in accordance with your own observations of their preferences, and knowledge of their particular biological requirements.

GROUP 3

Semi-terrestrial temperate turtles

This group features North American species such as Wood turtles and Box turtles. These animals all require continual access to drinking and bathing water, and prefer plenty of leafy or mossy undergrowth in which to hide and hunt for prey. Temperatures should be moderate (18°-26°C), and relatively high levels of humidity are often preferred. Neither Box turtles nor Wood turtles enjoy excessive exposure to heat and will often retreat and enter a state of aestivation (summer `hibernation') if conditions become too hot and dry. In America, both Box and Wood turtles are often referred to as marsh or forest turtles and this does convey a fairly accurate picture of their preferred habitats; shaded woodland groves, open woodland, damp river edges, the peripheries of marshes and low lying grassland - all are typical habitats of these shy and attractively marked turtles. Daytime and overnight temperatures are approximately the same as for North American terrestrial species.

Ornate Box turtle - Terrapene ornata

GROUP 4

Semi-terrestrial tropical turtles

This group includes a number of South American and Asiatic species. Some are rarely seen in captivity, but others such as Asiatic Box turtles of the genus *Cuora* and S. American semi-terrestrial turtles such as *Rhinoclemys* species are quite frequently encountered.

In many ways, the habitats of these tropical turtles closely mirror those of their temperate cousins; the principal difference is to be found in the temperature range required. Genuinely tropical turtles favour much higher temperatures, generally in the order of 27°-30°C day and night. Humidity requirements are invariably on the very high side, and these turtles must never be allowed to dry out.

Cuora flavomarginata is an Asiatic Box turtle which inhabits ponds and flooded rice fields. It is a small species, rarely exceeding 150mm in length.

GROUP 5

Mainly aquatic temperate freshwater turtles

This group includes the most popular of all turtles to be kept as a pet, the North American Red-eared Slider (*Trachemys scripta elegans*). It also includes a number of less frequently seen turtles from the same region such as Map turtles (*Graptemys* spp.), Common or Alligator Snapping Turtles (*Chelydra serpentina* and *Macroclemys temmincki*), Soft-shell turtles (*Apalone/Trionyx* spp.) and both Musk and Mud turtles (*Sternotherus* spp. and *Kinosternon* spp.). Clearly, within such a range of species the fine detail of habitat preference differs considerably from one to another, but nonetheless all do share a basic tolerance to a cold winter and hot summer seasonal cycle. Whilst most of the temperate climate aquatic turtles sold in pet shops are of North American

HOUSING TORTOISES & TURTLES

Accommodation requirements are obviously very different for each of the habitat groups discussed previously. All accommodation must be designed with the natural requirements of the particular species it is intended to house very firmly in mind. Some species require a lot of space (*e.g* Leopard tortoises) whilst others are relatively undemanding in this respect (*e.g* Box turtles); some prefer dry conditions whilst others require a high level of ambient humidity. In each case however, their basic needs in captivity are similar to those in the wild, and keepers must be prepared to invest time and effort to ensure that all accommodation is of the highest possible standard and meets their biological requirements.

GROUP 1

Mediterranean tortoises

Mediterranean tortoises all require a reasonably sized outdoor area comprising part overgrown borders or weedy patches, part open lawn, part harder surfaced patio or rocky area and part raised area (such as a rockery). This will provide sunny locations for basking, retreats from the heat in very hot weather, plenty of interest and even some naturally occurring food such as weeds and grass.

Small pens on lawns are categorically *not* suitable *or* humane. Tortoises must have an interesting, varied territory with sufficient space to roam, bask or graze. Security is important. Tortoises are excellent climbers and diggers and this must be considered when designing accommodation. These days, tortoise thefts are also a very real problem and so it may well be worth-while fitting a security alarm in your installation - the PIR (Passive Infra-Red) detector type is probably the best. A couple of these will protect quite a large area at moderate cost.

The perimeter should be opaque, not see-through. If tortoises can see through it (*e.g* wire mesh) then they will constantly be trying to climb over it or break through. If it is opaque (*e.g* plywood) then this will not happen. We use 18mm industrial quality plywood sawn into 2m long x 450mm high sections,

reinforced with battens and bolted together. This is fitted all around each and every tortoise enclosure giving a very high degree of escape-proofing. So far, it has proved 100% effective against even the most determined escape artists!

For evening use, tortoises should be provided with a dry, well protected house; again, ours are made out of thick plywood. These are raised slightly off the ground and are entered by ramps. They are much appreciated by all of the tortoises.

In prolonged periods of very bad weather, a greenhouse can be very useful; however, in the case of North African tortoises special care must be taken to ensure that the humidity level does not fall too low - these animals prefer a semi-humid environment with good ventilation. Turkish and Greek origin tortoises such as *Testudo hermanni* and *Testudo ibera* are much more tolerant of very hot, dry and dusty conditions. If North African tortoises however are exposed to similar conditions then runny noses and respiratory complaints often follow. In the wild, when conditions become too dry, these tortoise aestivate by digging a burrow in the sand or soil - this maintains localised humidity around the nasal passages. These conditions are very difficult to replicate in captivity, and it is best to avoid subjecting tortoises to conditions which require this mode of behaviour.

Some additional heating can be extremely useful during the occasional periods of bad weather experienced both early and late in the year; for *Testudo hermanni* and *Testudo ibera* a simple infra-red heater or 100W spotlamp suspended about 50cm above ground level is quite suitable. This provides quite good basking facilities.

This method however is *not* well suited to North African species which often develop nasal discharges and other respiratory symptoms if maintained in this way. For these species, we prefer a less direct and more subtle heat source. Generalised background heating to about 22°C provided by electric tubular heaters, combined with a moderate level of ambient humidity, is much safer and more effective. Some basking facilities are provided, but are placed higher above the ground than for use with *T. hermanni*. This appears to suit the tortoises quite well, and certainly reduces the incidence of environmentally induced nose and eye problems.

It should be noted that in all cases high temperatures should *not* be maintained overnight, but allowed to fall naturally. If high temperatures are maintained overnight this can cause quite serious metabolic and especially digestive upsets. Minimum overnight temperatures should not fall below 10°C however for Mediterranean tortoises. In really cold weather, such as in early spring or autumn when ground frosts are common, some form of overnight background heating is essential for safety. Alternatively, always bring tortoises into the house overnight early and later on in the year.

An outdoor terrarium suitable for juvenile Mediterranean tortoises.

GROUP 2

Tropical tortoises

Tropical tortoises have very different requirements from temperate species (from areas which naturally experience a summer-winter cycle). In tropical areas, the differences between summer and winter weather range from moderate or slight to none at all. Certain species come from semi-tropical areas (*e.g* Leopard tortoises) whilst others come from totally tropical areas (*e.g* Redfoot tortoises). Generally speaking, the more truly tropical the country of origin the more constantly warm and humid the environment required. Both Leopard tortoises (*G.pardalis*) and Bell's Hingeback tortoise (*K. belliana*) have a very wide natural distribution and in much of that zone do experience a cold dry season (usually between April

and September). During this period Hingeback tortoises are often to be found in old termite mounds or in burrows which they scrape into earth embankments; Leopard tortoises prefer to sit out the bad weather under a protective bush.

All tropical and semi-tropical tortoises will require extensive indoor artificially heated accommodation for at least some of the year. *They cannot, under any circumstances, be treated as temperate or Mediterranean tortoises.* This requirement must be carefully considered when deciding whether or not to keep such demanding animals in the first place.

It is possible in captivity to replicate the `cold dry season' but this is an exacting, very critical business and if you are thinking of doing so you should seek first hand advice from experienced keepers of these species.

Small specimens and juveniles will live quite happily in a large, well lit and heated vivarium; we use standardised vivaria made from plywood measuring approximately 2m x 600mm x 600mm for hatchlings and juveniles. These are heated by a 300W tubular heater operated via a thermostat. Background temperatures are maintained at about 22°C day and night. In addition a `hot-spot' is also essential to encourage basking and correct thermoregulation. Either a 100W spot lamp or a 100W infra-red ceramic heater may be used on a vivarium of this size. Temperatures directly under the basking heater should be around 28°C.

For some **tropical tortoises** (for example, Hingeback and Redfoot tortoises) the vivarium temperatures need to be more stable and a little higher - we keep ours at a constant temperature of about 22°-26°C day and night.

Lighting is also very important. Some tropical species such as Leopard tortoises need very strong bright light in order to feed well. We use and recommend True-lite® and Sun-Glo® full spectrum fluorescent tubes for this purpose. These tubes are excellent for all reptile applications and provide not only a very good replica of natural daylight, but also some essential Ultra Violet. Our standard vivaria will take a 48" 40W fitting. Other suitable tubes include Triton or Northlight . We must stress that adequate lighting and heating systems of the type described are not optional - they are absolutely essential if Leopard and similar tropical species are to survive captivity in good health.

Some Redfoot and Hingeback tortoises however do not like bright light, and tend to prefer a much lower lighting intensity - we use only a single 48" tube in our Redfoot and Hingeback vivaria and we have very reduced basking facilities compared to that provided for the Leopard tortoises. It is also useful to know that Hingeback and Redfoot tortoises often prefer to feed at dawn or dusk, when light levels are low. As always however, observe your tortoises' behaviour closely and adjust these suggested guide-lines in accordance with their reactions. Good tortoise keepers do not follow printed instructions slavishly, but interpret them in the light of their own observations.

Vivaria are fine for small specimens, but given the very rapid growth of certain of these species (especially Redfoot and Leopard tortoises) they do not remain small for long! To give an example,

Manouria emys (Burmese Brown tortoise). This truly tropical species is the largest Asiatic land tortoise reaching carapace lengths in excess of 50cm and weights in excess of 30kg.

within as little as 12 months a Leopard tortoise juvenile can increase in weight from 300g to over 2kg - in another 12 months, the same tortoise could weigh 4kg. The growth of Redfoot tortoises tends to be less dramatic, but adults still require a lot of space. Other large species expand just as rapidly; for example, we have seen *Geochelone sulcata* (the African Spurred tortoise) more than double in length and weight within 6 months. Such growth rates impose a considerable strain upon the resources of their keeper; not merely in terms of the space required but also in respect of heating and feeding bills. A 30kg tortoise is an expensive proposition in more ways than one!

Accommodation for large specimens should consist of a fairly extensive indoor pen; at least 3.5m x 3.5m square. Once again adequate lighting and heating systems must be suspended above it. This will provide accommodation throughout most of the year

when the weather is not warm enough for them to venture outside.

In warm weather tropical tortoises should also be allowed outside. Some species such as Redfoot tortoises and Hingeback tortoises will require a thickly vegetated area with plenty of cover. Leopard tortoises will prefer wider open spaces with plenty of weeds and grass upon which to graze.

Once again, converted greenhouses or garden sheds can provide good quality accommodation for tropical tortoises. Fitted out with appropriate heaters and some additional lighting for use overwinter, they are certainly to be recommended and make a much more pleasant environment than an indoor vivarium. The lower panes of glass should be replaced or lined with sheets of plywood - both to provide additional security and to prevent the tortoises from trying continually to walk through them. Our own Leopard tortoises are housed in a 2m x 2m square greenhouse with the lower half consisting of wooden frames - we have had to substantially strengthen this several times as these very large tortoises have demonstrated an inclination to force their way right through the lower frames, ripping out nails, screws and 20mm thick planking as if it were tissue paper! We have found that a simple surface-mounted outdoor terrarium made of wood with a polycarbonate 'Twinwall' roofing sheet for a top provides a good form of housing for many medium-sized tropical species.

GROUP 3

Temperate semi-terrestrial turtles

This group includes *Terrapene carolina* (the Box turtle), *Clemmys insculpta* (the Wood turtle) and *Clemmys guttata* (the Spotted turtle).

All *Terrapene carolina* sub-species enjoy warm (but not too hot) conditions with a very high level of humidity. Summer thunderstorms are perfect, and a thorough soaking is considered a real treat! In very hot and dry weather Box turtles become inactive, and in the wild actually aestivate (summer `hibernation') disappearing for weeks on end. Although this is obviously satisfactory in the wild, it is not easy in captivity to provide safe locations and conditions for such behaviour; it should not therefore be encouraged. If adequate humidity is present, aestivation should not occur.

Our own colony of Box turtles live outside from

spring to early autumn in a 2m x 2m secure wooden frame which is heavily planted to retain moisture and which has plenty of semi-rotting logs and rocks to provide cover and hunting grounds. No artificial

American Box turtles will enjoy a near natural environment if one is provided. Health problems are much reduced under such conditions.

light or heat is provided throughout the warm spring and summer months and our Box turtle unit is located in a partly-shaded position underneath a tree. It receives the sun mainly in the early morning and late afternoon. Any such unit needs to be totally secure and escape-proof; Box turtles can climb and dig very effectively indeed. Half of our frame is covered with welded wire mesh and the other half is glazed. The collection thrives under such conditions with regular breeding activity.

Box turtles do not like and cannot tolerate excessive radiant heat or constant exposure to bright light. If maintained in `dry' vivarium conditions serious eye and respiratory conditions will result. *Often these conditions can be cured simply by correcting the environment.*

A pool of drinking water big enough for the turtles to immerse in is essential. Outdoor and indoor terraria should always include such a facility. It is important that the water is clean and is changed regularly; if not, then it will rapidly accumulate bacteria and parasitic organisms which will eventually infect the turtles using the pool. Small cartridge filters can usually be adapted to use in Box turtle ponds. These will certainly help with water hygiene.

Clemmys species require very similar conditions, but are more generally aquatic. A much larger pond area is therefore essential for these turtles. Of the *Clemmys* group, *Clemmys insculpta*, the Wood turtle, is by far the most terrestrial in habit but even so continuous access to a good sized shallow pond is vital. Box turtles too will often swim if given the opportunity, so if at all possible do provide them with a suitably sized pond.

In addition to the outdoor area, a gently heated greenhouse or humid vivarium is also essential to provide alternative accommodation during long spells of really bad weather or over the winter period. One member of this group, *Clemmys muhlenbergi* or the Bog turtle, is extremely endangered throughout its entire range and most definitely must not be collected, traded in or kept as a pet by private individuals. What this turtle really needs more than anything (in common with many others), is for its primary habitat to be protected from human `developers'.

GROUP 4

Tropical & temperate aquatic turtles

Most of these turtles are well suited to a vivarium environment, although in some cases outdoor accommodation can be utilised during the warm summer months. Because these are all relatively small species, it is usually possible to base the vivarium around standard tropical fish tanks - however, only large ones are usually suitable. The minimum I would normally consider satisfactory for a fully grown adult pair of Red-eared terrapins for example is 2m long x 500mm wide. This should be 50/50 to 75/25 land and water in most cases.

Lighting

All indoor terrapin tanks or ponds will require some form of artificial lighting. Ordinary tungsten light bulbs are not suitable by themselves but they can provide a useful source of basking heat and their low colour temperature (orange-yellow) also appears to encourage basking. We recommend the use of 60W or 100W reflector spot lamps for basking purposes. For the main light source the best system by far is True-lite, a fluorescent system which offers a remarkably good approximation of natural daylight. True-lite® tubes are available in various sizes from 18" to 6' (460mm to 2m approx) so one should certainly suit your system. The benefits of this type of lighting are two-fold; the colour temperature of the light is $5,500^\circ K$ which is close to natural daylight thus encouraging natural activity and behavioural patterns and in addition these tubes also emit some Ultra-Violet radiation which is important as it contributes to the natural production of Vitamin D3 (essential to healthy bone development). U.V is blocked by glass, so even if a tank is placed in a brightly lit window position this is not by itself adequate. A U.V emitting tube such as True-lite® will provide the missing component indoors. In practice, if a multi-vitamin and mineral supplement such as Vionate© or Nutrobal® is used regularly it is highly unlikely that any D3 deficiency will occur. Even so, the overall benefits of a Full Spectrum Lighting system are enormous and I would regard it as an essential component of any exclusively indoor maintenance system. Not merely on account of their U.V output, but rather because they so closely approximate the colour temperature of natural daylight and therefore do tend to reduce stress and encourage normal behaviour. Where non-FSL lighting is used, I have noted an increased tendency to lethargy and inactivity.

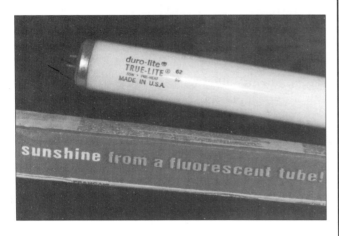

Full Spectrum Lighting tubes are recommended for all tortoise and turtle vivaria in indoor installations.

Heating

General warmth can be provided by a combination of undertank heater-thermostats and overhead basking lamps (60W should be adequate in most cases for the latter). The air humidity should be medium-high, but certainly not saturated; make sure that there is good ventilation at all times. Sub-soil heating pads can also be useful.

For most North American turtles, which are the kinds most often kept as pets, the water temperature should be maintained in the range 23°C to 29°C. Excessively high temperatures (over 32°C) or prolonged periods at too low a temperature (less than 20°C) can be dangerous.

A word on normal fishtank type heater-thermostats. These are obviously electrical devices and it is well known that electricity and water is not a good combination. Many heater-thermostats are also encased in glass; this is fine in the tranquil surroundings of a tropical fish tank but an aggressive terrapin or rampaging Snapping turtle can soon cause untold damage. In my experience their casing can all too easily be fractured allowing the water in the tank to become `live' - *this is a potentially lethal situation for owner and turtle alike.* A further hazard is that the heater may be used as a plaything and end up out of the water; should this occur it will certainly overheat and may become very dangerous. As a result of personally experiencing a couple of highly unpleasant incidents of this sort I would suggest adopting the following safety code in respect of all turtle heating and electrical installations:-

ALWAYS fit and use an Earth Leakage Circuit Breaker (ELCB) in all animal electrical applications; these are available at low cost from any electrical store. They sense if an electrical shock hazard situation has occurred and cut off the power instantly, before a lethal charge results. They can represent the difference between life and death and in my opinion it is extremely foolish not to make use of them.

DO NOT use glass-encased heaters or thermostats in turtle installations; they simply are not strong enough. If using any submersible heater, protect it by enclosing it in a secondary plastic or metal grill glued to the sides of the tank using aquarium sealant.

ANY HEATER which the turtles can touch may cause burns; the same applies to carelessly situated basking lamps. Be careful. Protect submersible heaters with a shield as advised above.

THE BEST heating system for aquatic turtle tanks consists of underfloor pads which at no time come into contact with the water. These are very effective and completely safe. They are usually controlled by a separate and easily adjustable electronic thermostat.

The water area of the tank must be deep enough for the terrapins to submerge themselves completely and to be able to swim freely. A land area is also required, and this is usually most conveniently located at one end of the tank. Easy access to the land area must be possible, a sloping ramp is usually the best approach. Beware, however, of fixtures and fittings under which terrapins could become trapped. This land area can consist of submerged bricks supporting a peat and gravel surface layer. To prevent this becoming saturated with water, the land area can be constructed in a large plastic tray. Above this a 100W spot lamp should be positioned to provide artificial basking facilities.

Overcrowding in tanks is a major contributory factor in the incidence of disease. It is far better to under-stock a tank than to over-stock it. A tank which is crowded will rapidly become fouled and quite probably smelly and unpleasant - for both the terrapins and their keeper. Good filtration helps, but is not a substitute for common sense in stocking; and remember, small terrapins can grow very quickly. As a general guide, the maximum recommended stocking capacity of a tank can be decided using the following formula:

$$\frac{\text{Surface area of tank : Length of terrapins}}{982 \text{ sq cm : } 10 \text{ cm}}$$

Or, more approximately, every 1000sq cm of surface area allows for a maximum of 10cm carapace length of terrapin. In this case, 2 terrapins of 5cm each or 1 terrapin of 10cm.

To give another example, a typical 60 x 30 cm tank has a surface area of 1800sq cm and so could accommodate two terrapins each measuring up to 9cm in carapace length or three each measuring up to 6cm long.

Land area

The land surface of an aquatic terrarium should comprise both soil and gravel. This is essential; decorations may then be added in the form of logs and plants. These not only look attractive but they provide cover and an important sense of security for the turtles.

Plants & decorations

A selection of plants in the turtle vivarium (both terrestrial and aquatic) look absolutely splendid, of that there is no doubt. What is in doubt is how long they will last. Turtles will often eat these 'decorations', or may simply use them as toys and destroy them. In a large tank or pond, the natural ability of the plants to recover might - just might - enable them to survive. Aquatic plants can definitely help to improve and sustain water quality, but their practical downside is that they can very easily harbour pests and parasites and are virtually impossible to sterilise. Artificial, plastic plants are actually quite useful accessories. They provide good cover, look very attractive, and are easy to sterilise. Choose tough looking ones - fragile varieties will last

no time at all. A good compromise is to use a combination of real and artificial plants; the real ones provide water quality enhancement and something for the turtles to nibble, and should be changed regularly. The plastic ones provide secure long-term hiding places which need not be disturbed unless cleaning is required. If turtles do consistently bite pieces out of plastic plant decorations, a potential hazard exists; such material can lead to gut impactions. In these cases, the plants are best dispensed with. However, most turtles and plastic plants co-exist quite happily.

Water area

The water section in most tanks does not need to be very deep - in the majority of cases 150-200mm will suffice, although larger turtles may require considerably more. Some turtles, most notably Soft-shell turtles, like to burrow into the tank bottom; we normally place a layer of sand and grit to a depth of

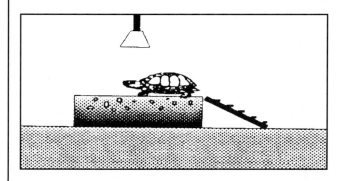

Above: The land area of an aquatic terrarium should allow easy access and is best situated under a basking heat source.

about 30-40mm depth on the tank base-plate so that they can express this natural behaviour. It is not true, by the way, that terrapins should be kept only in water no deeper than they are long; in the wild they are found in water several feet deep, and my own turtles live quite happily in a pond which is more than two feet deep. The main problem with keeping turtles in captivity is water hygiene. Turtles are messy feeders and for even a small specimen in a modest vivarium quite powerful filtration will be needed.

By far the best filters are external canister types which use a foam filtration medium; our own aquatic turtle tanks use Fluval model 403 or equivalent units from manufacturers such as Eheim. These ensure good water circulation and a high standard of water purity. Nothing is worse than dirty turtle water - it poses not only a health hazard to the turtles, but also - potentially - to their keepers. It is also very smelly and generally unpleasant. Use an effective filter and you will not only keep the water crystal clear but also reduce the manual labour and tedium of frequent water changes.

It is worth noting that what is actually required in a turtle set-up is good quality mechanical filtration; biological filtration as found in tropical fish aquaria is very difficult to achieve in chelonian installations and is rarely effective. The waste which needs to be removed is also far bulkier than that produced by fish and will soon clog up the fine filter `wool' supplied as standard with most filter units intended for fish. We remove this material and instead add extra foam or coarse granular media which is better suited to turtle maintenance conditions.

In our smaller turtle tanks we have found internal foam canister filters excellent at keeping the water clean. These are especially safe for hatchlings and small turtles who may find the turbulent water currents created by more powerful filters uncomfortable. If the foam media becomes clogged with waste, it is easily removed, given a quick rinse under the tap and then replaced. This should be done regularly, or whenever the flow of water through the filter diminishes as a result of waste accumulation.

Another way around the `dirty water' problem is to employ a separate feeding tank; however, this procedure is extremely time consuming, often messy, and obviously requires the filling and emptying of a separate tank or bowl each feeding session. This rapidly becomes a very unwelcome chore, which given the avoidance of overfeeding and provision of adequate filtration in the main tank system is completely unnecessary. I am also not keen on separate feeding tanks as they invariably involve a lot

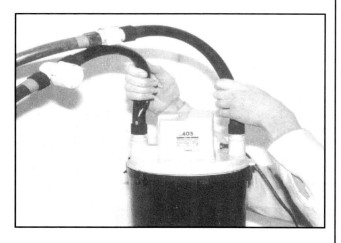

Large external canister filter suitable for use with turtle installations. For smaller tanks, a foam cartridge filter may be adequate.

of extra handling for the turtles which can result in stress.

Outdoor and indoor turtle ponds

Alternatives to glass aquarium tanks include indoor or outdoor ponds. Indoor ponds can be extremely attractive and successful, the only drawback being the space required. If the space is available, then they can make a very decorative display feature as well as providing an ideal home for several large terrapins. The framework of the pond can be constructed from wood and then lined with a heavy duty plastic pond liner, or alternatively may be made entirely from fibreglass. Equipped with a waterfall or fountain, and with the surrounding area well planted such a display is most impressive. Outdoor ponds can also be used but the construction of these is obviously a major undertaking. One end of the pond should slope gently to provide ease of access. A shallow area will also provide a differential temperature as it warms up under the sun more readily than the deeper end. The difference may only be 1°-2°C but this is sufficient to be noticed by the terrapins. A few logs partially submerged at other places will also provide not only exit points but also basking sites. All terrapins are excellent climbers and are adept at escaping, so good security around the pond area is vital. We suggest allowing at least 1m of ground area all around the pond, surrounded by a cement or brick wall at least 30cm high and further topped with wire mesh. Wire mesh should not be used on lower levels as the terrapins may injure themselves on it - claws can easily become stuck, and delicate noses abrade rather easily. Small terrapins may be viewed as prey by large birds (particularly herons), so these should not be released into open pond areas. Shelters should also be provided, and the surrounding area can be attractively planted. Outdoor ponds are therefore ideal if you have a large number of terrapins and sufficient garden space to permit installation.

Only hardy (temperate) terrapins can be kept out of doors, *tropical species from warm climates cannot be kept in this way.* Even temperate species will almost certainly require some form of supplementary water heating system on occasions. This form of accommodation is also not really suitable for juvenile or hatchling terrapins - only large and relatively robust adults can be kept in this way. Juveniles are best housed indoors in heated tanks, at least until they have attained a reasonable size.

Ponds intended for year-round use must be at least 1m in depth and must have a large surface area. Ponds which are deep, but which lack surface area, can result in dangerously low levels of oxygenation -

especially during hot weather or in the winter. Water oxygenation can be improved using waterfalls, fountains and external (Koi carp type) pond filters. In outdoor ponds, hardy turtles will hibernate during the cold winter months. Whilst hibernating they do not surface to breath air, but instead absorb oxygen through their skin. In order to avoid anoxia (oxygen starvation), it is vitally important that the pond is adequately oxygenated at all times. *Unless you are absolutely certain that your pond is entirely suitable it is usually much safer to overwinter the turtles indoors in properly heated tanks.*

It is also important that the pond has a good bottom layer of mud and other sediment as this will be used by the hibernating terrapins for protection from extreme cold. Total freezing of the surface in winter can be prevented by using submersible pond-warmers. These and many other accessories can be obtained from water-garden centres and aquatic mail order suppliers. The catalogues issued by aquatic supply companies can provide a wealth of interesting ideas and often contain many useful items which used imaginatively can greatly improve the quality of a captive turtle's life.

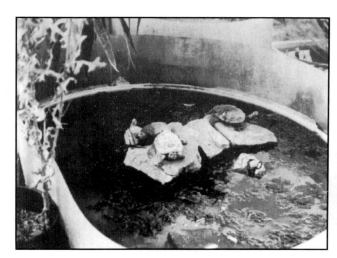

Left

Plastic garden ponds can be surface mounted outdoors to provide a very satisfactory alternative to indoor tanks for temperate species. Escapes can be prevented by surrounding the pond with tall fibreglass flexible sheeting.

Right

Provision of an adequate basking area is vital in both pond and indoor vivarium environments. Water quality is also critical, so ensure regular water changes and good filtration.

23

KEEPING TURTLES OUTDOORS

Above

This outdoor accommodation unit provides a secure home for a group of semi-aquatic turtles; it includes a warm transparent plastic covered section, a small pond, and a predator-proof and escape-proof mesh covered area.

Right

American Box turtles are well suited to the type of accommodation shown above. In cold weather however, they may require some extra heating (this depends very much upon where you live).

Always aim to provide a secure but interesting environment for your tortoises and turtles. Outdoor units offer many advantages for suitable species. Even tropical species can often be kept out of doors for part of the year. Be sure to investigate the exact requirements of the particular species you keep. High quality housing makes life better not only for the animals, but enhances the pleasure of keeping them for the owner.

HIBERNATION

Most land tortoises of the types commonly kept as pets (in Europe these are generally Mediterranean species; in the USA, Box turtles and Gopher tortoises are more often seen) do actually hibernate in the wild. They do so however for a much shorter period than that to which are often subjected in captivity. It has frequently been commonplace to hibernate these tortoises in captivity for six or even seven months, whereas in the wild the same tortoises would experience a hibernation rarely longer than ten to twelve weeks - often much less. Some very small tortoises from the warm coastal zones of Tunisia and Libya only hibernate for a month or so, and in mild winters some do not hibernate at all. Instead, certain of these tortoises **aestivate** - disappearing underground for a couple of months in the middle of the summer to escape the extreme heat. They resurface again in late summer or early autumn; quite a different life cycle from tortoises in other parts of the Mediterranean. Although superficially similar to hibernation, aestivation is physiologically a quite different process however.

We believe in replicating natural conditions as closely as possible as regards hibernation periods, and so we do not recommend giving your tortoise an over-long hibernation. Most fatalities occur either near the beginning, or at the end of the hibernation period. The reasons for some of these fatalities will be discussed later, but you can certainly improve your tortoises chances greatly simply by limiting the period of hibernation to not more than 20 weeks at the outside. This, it should be stressed, is for a perfectly fit specimen which is fully up to weight. Tortoises which are anything less than 100% fit, or are in any way underweight, will require a much shorter period of hibernation under carefully controlled conditions; possibly they may even need keeping awake and feeding over the entire winter season.

Most temperate aquatic turtles also hibernate in the wild and this can likewise be achieved in captivity; however, it is a relatively advanced procedure requiring a good deal of specialist knowledge and experience on the part of the keeper. There is little or no room for error. Our advice in most cases is to overwinter these animals. In the wild, such turtles usually hibernate in the mud on the bottom of rivers or ponds, but even where the animals are kept in a pond in captivity, it is highly unlikely to be able to provide conditions ideal for such a hibernation; anoxia, or lack of oxygen, is only one of several possible problems which can arise. For safety's sake, unless you are absolutely sure of what you are doing, we would caution against attempts at hibernating any aquatic turtle.

The following information applies therefore to the most common species of `pet' tortoise encountered in Europe; *Testudo graeca* and *Testudo hermanni*. Almost identical hibernation conditions are also required by Gopher tortoises from the United States (*Xerobates* and *Gopherus* species), and although these are rarely if ever seen in Europe, many continue to be kept as pets in their native country. Certainly the overall temperature and health guide-lines provided for the Mediterranean species can also be followed with confidence in the case of Gopher tortoises.

Never ever attempt to hibernate a tortoise which you suspect is ill, or which is underweight. To put a sick or underweight tortoise into hibernation is to condemn it to certain death.

In order to survive hibernation in good condition, tortoises need to have built up sufficient reserves of body fat; this in turn stores vitamins and water. Without fat, vitamins and water tortoises die of starvation or dehydration. Adequate reserves of body fat are vital to tortoises in hibernation; they live off these reserves whilst asleep, and if the reserves run out too soon then the animal's body will begin to use up the fat contained within the muscles and internal organs, eventually these too will become exhausted.

Small tortoises, such as this Tunisian animal, can only withstand very short hibernation periods compared to larger animals. In the wild, this tortoise would not normally hibernate at all.

Should this occur the tortoise will simply die in hibernation.

Weigh tortoises carefully before, during and after hibernation.

Tortoise weight check

There are several ways of determining whether or not a tortoise has accumulated sufficient weight to survive hibernation; the most frequently used method is based around the `Jackson Ratio' graph. In essence, this graph indicates the average weights of healthy tortoises plotted against their lengths. The basic principle being that by comparison with weight-length data taken from known healthy specimens, a tortoise which is `at risk' can be readily identified.

There are a couple of important points to make about this system. Firstly, it can only be used as a guide with respect to *Testudo hermanni, Testudo graeca,* and *Testudo ibera;* it does **not apply at all** to any other species. For example, if a Marginated tortoise (*Testudo marginata*) is plotted against this graph, the result will be completely misleading; *T. marginata* have an unusually narrow and elongate body form compared to the species listed previously and consistently read `underweight' on the graph even though they may actually be up to a perfectly safe weight. To give another example, *Testudo horsfieldi* (Horsfield's tortoise) are very compact, broad and `stubby' in body-form; these tend to read overweight even though they may in fact be marginally underweight. So, the graph must be employed to assess only those species upon which it was based, and *it should not be used* (other than very generally) to assess *any other kind* of tortoise or turtle.

The second point to make is that the smaller the tortoise being assessed, the less room there is for any error in measurement. Various things can lead to false readings; these include the state of hydration and whether or not a female tortoise is carrying eggs.

If a tortoise urinates, or drinks, immediately prior to being weighed this can distort the readings considerably. The best weight measurement to use would be an average taken daily over, say, ten days. `Spot weight tests' based upon a single measurement are notoriously inaccurate. Tortoises can quite easily gain or lose 10% or more of their total bodyweight almost instantly as a result of drinking or urination.

Finally on the topic of weight, one sometimes hears that (whether for a hibernation weight check or for the purposes of prescribing drugs) a certain percentage of the body weight (often quoted as one-third) "does not count, to allow for the shell"; this is *not true.* In all cases the total bodyweight *must* be taken into account. The `shell' is, after all, living tissue and is every bit as much an integral part of the animal as its skin, muscle or indeed any other organ.

There is also frequent confusion about the correct way to measure the length of a tortoise; for the purposes of the weight graph the measurement required is the Straight Carapace Length (SCL). This is the total length of the tortoise, in a straight line, measured along the median line from nuchal to supracaudal. The length `over the curve' is not relevant to the pre-hibernation weight check.

With the length of the tortoise measured in millimetres, and the weight in grammes, check the status of the tortoise against the graph. If it is seriously underweight as indicated by the lower line, then under no circumstances should it be hibernated. Indeed, if it is plotted below the `average' (upper) line by any amount then serious consideration must be given as to whether or not it is fit to hibernate.

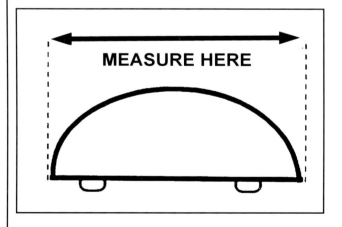

Above: The correct way to measure a tortoise's Straight Carapace Length (SCL). Measure in a straight line without curving the ruler over the shell.

HIBERNATION HEALTH CHECK LIST

Before preparing your tortoise for its winter hibernation, it is essential that some basic health checks are undertaken; if a sick tortoise is subjected to hibernation it will almost certainly not survive. These checks should be performed with great care, and any abnormal results reported to your veterinary surgeon immediately. Carefully check:

BOTH EYES for signs of swelling, inflammation or discharge. If there is a problem, consult a veterinary surgeon with experience of treating reptile patients.

THE NOSE for signs of discharge; a persistently runny nose requires urgent veterinary investigation. Tortoises with this symptom must also be isolated from contact with others, as some varieties of R.N.S. ('Runny Nose Syndrome') are highly contagious. The presence of excess mucus also encourages bacterial growth, and hence places the tortoise in additional danger from diseases such as necrotic stomatitis.

THE TAIL for inflammation or internal infection; tortoises with cloacitis 'leak' from the tail and smell strongly. Any signs of abnormality should be investigated by a veterinary surgeon. It will help if you take a fresh sample of cloacal excretion for examination under the microscope.

THE LEGS for any unusual lumps or swellings; abscesses are common in reptiles and if left untreated can result in loss of limb or even death. Report any unusual findings to a veterinary surgeon who may want to X-ray the affected part.

BOTH EARS which should be either flat or slightly concave; ear abscesses are very common and can have fatal consequences if treatment is not obtained. The ear flaps, the tympanic membranes, are the two large 'scales' just behind the jaw-bone.

INSIDE THE MOUTH for any sign of abnormality; Necrotic Stomatitis or 'Mouth-rot' is a highly contagious (and unfortunately all too common) disease of captive reptiles. It is characterised by the appearance of a yellow 'cheesy' substance in the mouth, or by a deep red-purple tinge, or by the appearance of small blood-spots. Sometimes all three symptoms are present. *Expert veterinary treatment is called for as a matter of urgency if the animal is to be saved.*

These basic checks in conjunction with the weight checks form your essential pre-hibernation examination. Provided your tortoise is up to weight and no other abnormalities can be detected, then you may begin preparation for hibernation. The golden rule at all times is if in doubt seek expert advice. Our experience is that owners who fail to act promptly when problems occur usually end up, sooner or later, with a dead tortoise or turtle.

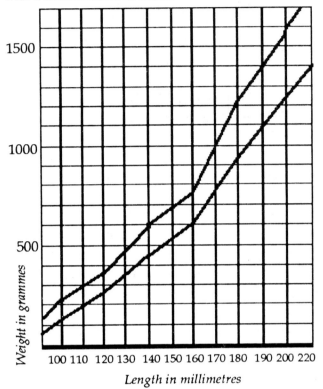

Weight-check graph for use with Testudo graeca. Read the carapace length from the bottom line of the chart in millimetres, the weight from the side in grammes.

One final and critically important point: very many tortoises die each year because owners attempt to hibernate them whilst they still contain undigested food matter in their stomach. It is natural for tortoises to gradually reduce their food intake as the autumn approaches (this is one reason why, if they are underweight in August, they will certainly not have put on any extra by October). A tortoise's digestive system is governed to a great extent by temperature but, generally speaking, when the tortoise's biological processes are slowing down it takes between 3-6 weeks for the food last consumed to pass through the gastrointestinal tract. The precise time taken depends upon the size of the tortoise and the ambient temperature. The larger the tortoise, and the lower the temperature, the longer this process takes. Bearing these factors in mind, it is generally advisable not to attempt to hibernate any tortoise if it has eaten within the last month. *Delay hibernation rather than allow a tortoise to hibernate whilst the possibility remains of undigested food matter within the upper intestine.*

Tortoises which are hibernated with undigested or partially digested food still remaining inside are unlikely to survive in good health. The food decays in the stomach and produces large quantities of gas which can result in a condition known as tympanitic colic which in turn can cause asphyxiation due to internal pressure on the lungs.

HIBERNATION AND OVERWINTERING OF BOX AND WOOD TURTLES

American Box turtles can and do hibernate in the wild and can also do so in captivity, but obviously light or underweight specimens must not be hibernated. Hibernation temperatures are as for Mediterranean species but a higher level of ambient humidity needs to be maintained. Slightly moist leaves, pine mulch, moss and earth are a good combination of media. A maximum of 3 months hibernation is recommended but only for 100% fit specimens. Others should be overwintered in a damp vivarium at between 17°C and 24°C. Avoid total reliance upon radiant heat - a good overall background warmth is far better for this species. Bright lights are not much liked and we find a 20W True-lite tube more than adequate. A small basking area can be provided for those specimens who wish to take advantage - we find 40W mini-spot lamps best for this. Beware of excessively drying out the vivarium however - a few hours a day basking time is more than adequate. The main problem is in keeping everything sufficiently wet. *Plenty of moss, dead leaves and rotting wood can certainly help in this respect.* A hand sprayer filled with water, as used for house plants, can also help to provide an adequate level of humidity and prevent over-drying. If the correct environment is attained, then Box, Wood or similar semi-terrestrial turtles will continue to feed well and behave normally throughout the winter months.

HIBERNATION DANGERS

The two biggest killers of hibernating tortoises in captivity are:-

- **Attempting to hibernate unfit or underweight specimens**
- **Failure to provide adequate protection during hibernation**

Hopefully you have taken note of the advice given on fitness for hibernation and so will avoid this problem. However, even fit tortoises can die in hibernation if the conditions to which they are subjected are biologically incorrect. Essentially this means:-

- **Keeping the tortoise dry and well insulated in properly prepared accommodation.**
- **Making absolutely certain that temperatures are stable, and within safe tolerances, i.e neither too hot nor too cold.**

In practice the first is the more easily accomplished. We will deal with both accommodation and conditions separately, and in some detail.

Accommodation during hibernation

Our recommendation is for an outer box or carton made from either wood or substantial cardboard - a tea-chest is absolutely perfect. The inside of this should be lined with blocks or chippings of polystyrene, of the sort used in house insulation or packaging. Alternatively, tightly packed shredded paper can be used. Straw is also satisfactory but should remain a third choice as it can harbour mould spores and other potentially irritant substances.

Select a second (this time much smaller) box. Ideally this box should accommodate the tortoise fairly tightly, whilst still allowing for a couple of inches of insulating material all around the animal.

It may be asked why two individual boxes are necessary. To answer this question one has only to

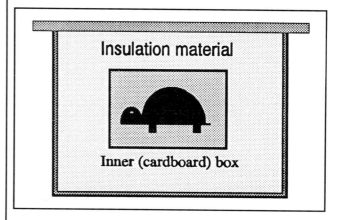

monitor carefully the behaviour of a hibernating tortoise. A tortoise in hibernation often does not remain entirely inert, but might attempt to move; it may either dig deeper into its box or climb to the surface. If it is allowed unrestrained movement there is a grave danger that it may burrow through the protective insulating layers and come into contact with the walls of the hibernation box. Here, it is virtually unprotected, and *could easily freeze to death in a very short while if the surrounding temperature falls too low*. In the spring, following a severe winter, our Sanctuary Hospital is often full of frozen tortoises due to precisely this error on the part of owners. It is all rather sad and unnecessary as the problem is so easily avoided with just a little care.

Environmental conditions during hibernation

The most important factor is the temperature. Maintenance of a safe temperature is absolutely critical to a successful and healthy hibernation. Insulation merely slows down the rate of heat exchange, it does not prevent it altogether. Therefore, no matter how well you insulate, if you subject your tortoise's hibernation box to sub-zero temperatures for an extended period it will **still get too cold**. Similarly, if you allow your tortoise's hibernation box to get too warm it will begin to use up valuable fat and energy reserves, and may even wake up early.

The critical temperatures for hibernation are:

> **MAXIMUM = 50°F or 10°C**
> **MINIMUM = 32°F or 0°C**

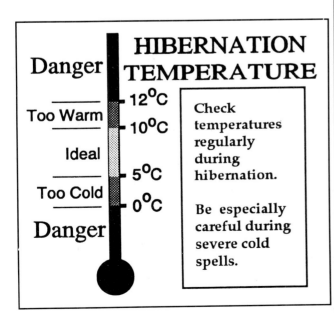

Danger	**HIBERNATION TEMPERATURE**
Too Warm — 12°C — 10°C	**Check temperatures regularly during hibernation.**
Ideal — 5°C	
Too Cold — 0°C	**Be especially careful during severe cold spells.**
Danger	

Under *no circumstances whatsoever should a hibernating tortoise be subjected to prolonged exposure to temperatures higher or lower than these.* Failure to appreciate the importance of this invariably leads to death and injury in hibernation. Blindness due to the eyes quite literally freezing solid is a particularly unpleasant consequence of allowing temperatures to fall too low.

The easiest and most accurate way to check temperatures is to obtain a maximum-minimum reading greenhouse thermometer from any garden or D.I.Y. shop. *Check it at regular intervals, hourly if necessary in very cold spells.* If sustained low or high temperatures are noted, temporarily move the tortoise into a more suitable place until temperatures stabilise to a satisfactory level again. Today, low cost digital electronic thermometers are available with built-in alarms which emit a 'bleep' if the temperature goes outside pre-set points. *These are truly excellent, and can make a major contribution to hibernation safety.*

An ideal temperature for hibernation is 5°C, or 40°F. At this temperature tortoises remain safely asleep, using minimal energy, but are in no danger of freezing. Incidentally, it is important to point out that the advice that a hibernating tortoise should never be disturbed is completely invalid. It has absolutely no basis in biological or veterinary science, and should be ignored. *You cannot possibly harm a hibernating tortoise simply by handling it.*

We routinely handle our tortoises during hibernation in order to check them; provided the animals are carefully replaced in their protective insulation, this is an excellent method of checking on their general condition. Most healthy adult tortoises lose about 1% of their body weight each month in hibernation. This is very easy to calculate. A 1600g tortoise put into hibernation in October will lose about 16g every month. After 5 of months hibernation it will probably weigh 1600 minus 5 x 16 = 80, *i.e* 1520g.

Whilst tortoises must not be put into hibernation with a stomach containing food matter, their bladders should contain some fluid. Therefore tortoises should be encouraged to drink before hibernation, even though they are not allowed to feed.

If, when checking a hibernating tortoise, you notice that it has urinated, get it up immediately and do not put it back. Recent evidence leads us to believe that should this occur, the animal is in grave danger of death from sudden, acute dehydration. If this action does occur, begin rehydration immediately, and overwinter for the remaining hibernation period. We are undertaking further research into this behaviour, but present results indicate that the problem is most likely to occur towards the end of the hibernation period or in spells of unusually mild weather where the temperature rises above 10°C or 50°F. Check the tortoise regularly at such times.

Modern electronic digital thermometers are highly accurate and are available at surprisingly low cost from hobby electronic stores or photographic processing dealers. They are ideal for both hibernation and incubation!

NATURAL (OR OUTDOOR) HIBERNATION

Outdoor or natural hibernation consists of allowing the tortoise to excavate its own burrow instead of hibernating it in a box under controlled conditions. In the wild tortoises usually dig themselves in under large rocks, tree roots, or into the side of earthen ledges. Excavations may be several feet deep. Some species, such as *Testudo horsfieldi*, excavate burrows that are several meters long.

Natural hibernation offers some advantages, and some disadvantages. In its favour, freezing is very unlikely to occur - even under severe weather conditions - as at anything beyond a few inches underground temperatures are very stable indeed. Even in the most severe weather, frosts rarely penetrate more than 2 inches deep. If your tortoise has safely hibernated itself in this way before, then there is no necessity to vary its routine. Natural hibernation is not intrinsically dangerous. The disadvantages of the method, however, include:-

- **Flooding. If this should occur, then the tortoise is at serious risk;**
- **Health inspections during hibernation are practically impossible;**
- **There is always the danger of attack by foxes, badgers or rodents.**

Bearing these possible problem areas in mind, you can do much to minimise the dangers.

Do not allow tortoises to burrow in an area where flooding is possible * Perform extra-careful health checks throughout the summer and especially during the period immediately prior to hibernation * The area above a hibernating tortoise can be protected by covering the ground with wire mesh - but be watch out in warm weather as the tortoise may be trying to emerge!

OVERWINTERING TORTOISES

Sometimes for health reasons hibernation may not be possible. Where this is the case, the objective must be to keep the animal alert, feeding and in good general condition throughout the winter period. Provided that temperatures are adequate, and that both food and light are also available in sufficient quantity and quality, over-wintering tortoises artificially is not particularly difficult.

Suitable accommodation must of course be provided. This can take several forms, but by far the easiest accommodation for just one or two tortoises is a medium sized vivarium. The instructions given earlier in respect of accommodation for tropical tortoises should be consulted for information on what is required.

We use large indoor open-topped pens when we have to overwinter a number of tortoises. Once again adequate heat and light are essential. Most of our pens have several 200 watt lights suspended above them, including several FSL(Full Spectrum Lighting) or True-lite tubes, in addition to infra-red heaters and other environmental control systems. As substrate material to line the base of the tank or pen, we recommend ordinary newspaper. This is cheap, hygienic, and easy to dispose of. It should be changed whenever it becomes soiled. Pine bark chippings can also be used and provide a more attractive flooring. They are also quite absorbent, but as with all `natural' substrates are not easy to sterilise. If this approach is adopted they must be changed very frequently otherwise parasitic and bacterial organisms will soon build up to dangerous concentrations.

Some North African tortoises can react very badly to dry, poorly ventilated vivaria. Respiratory disease due to irritation caused by incorrect levels of humidity can also result, although recently it has become clear that a highly contagious pathogen is also implicated. With these species, an open indoor pen, as described, is far better than vivarium tanks and even then great care must be taken to ensure excellent ventilation at all times.

It is essential to keep overwintering tortoises eating, to maintain both weight and a safe body-fluid balance. In order to feed well a daytime temperature in the region of 27°-28°C (80°-85°F) is required. Directly under the basking lamp ground temperatures should be somewhat higher, in the region of 32°C . You should always keep a thermometer in the vivarium area to ensure that these temperatures are achieved and maintained. Most tortoises from Mediterranean type habitats require a **temperature gradient** in order to function properly, *not just a constant all-round heat.* Typically, a suitable gradient would be from 32°C, directly under the main heat source, to 20°C in the `cool' section of the pen or vivarium. This gradient is extremely important to the tortoise, and helps it to maintain a number of vital body functions. Unless it is available, stress and other serious problems will almost certainly manifest.

It is important to emphasise that no matter how warm it is, an ordinary room in a house will not by itself keep a tortoise feeding and in good health over the long winter period. A combination of background heat, localised radiated heat, and high intensity illumination is absolutely essential. The tortoise requires this `spot' or radiant heat source to thermoregulate properly and to maintain its own body temperature (when measured in the cloaca) at around 2°-3°C above that of the surrounding area. It does this by heat absorption, rather like a dark coloured stone absorbs a great deal of heat from the sun.

At night the tortoise can be removed from its daytime accommodation and placed in a warm box situated next to a radiator to sleep. Again, it is important not to let it get too cold, certainly not below about 9°-10°C. In the morning replace it in its warm area for the day. *Tortoises need approximately 12-14 hours of adequate heat and light per day in order to feed properly and remain in good health.*

You can help your tortoise considerably by providing a dietary vitamin and mineral supplement regularly, this is particularly important when overwintering, as all recommended supplements contain vitamin D3 which is usually synthesised from sunlight.

This is perhaps an appropriate place to remark on **vitamin injections**. Unless the tortoise is suffering from a specific vitamin deficiency disease, injections are not recommended. *Certainly we do not approve of `routine' vitamin injections before hibernation.* If a tortoise is truly vitamin-deficient at this point - and barring serious illness, this is extremely unlikely if it has been given a reasonable diet - then do not hibernate it. Injections will not cure the problem. It is far better to build up vitamin and mineral stores gradually by providing a well balanced diet, and sprinkling a multi-vitamin/mineral preparation on the food regularly throughout the year. Genuine cases of acute vitamin deficiency in tortoises are actually quite rare; it is usually only found in those which have been subjected to an extremely poor diet over a very long period or where the tortoise is otherwise ill. Vitamin injections in any case *do not* help tortoises to survive hibernation. This is accomplished by good husbandry alone. Excessive and routine use of injections does however often cause local injection-site abscesses; all the more reason then to avoid them unless they really are necessary to treat a specific clinical condition.

One final point. Dehydration is a particular problem of overwintering, and should be avoided by providing your tortoise with a daily opportunity to drink. For details on how tortoises can best be encouraged to drink see below.

AFTER HIBERNATION

As the average ambient temperature begins to approach the critical point of 10°C or 50°F, a tortoise's metabolism will begin to reactivate in readiness for waking. Certain complex chemical and biological processes are initiated as the animal prepares to emerge into the spring sunshine. At this point unfortunately, it often runs into its first problem. In many countries where tortoises (originally from warm climates) are kept as pets, spring is often cold, wet, and miserable.

For humans, this sort of weather may be merely unpleasant. For tortoises it can present rather more serious problems. On first emerging from hibernation a tortoise is depleted in strength, has a low white blood cell (WBC) count and is very vulnerable to infection. Unless it receives adequate quantities of heat and light it will simply 'not get going properly', and instead of starting to regain the weight and strength lost during hibernation, may well refuse to eat, and begin to decline.

This condition in its most serious form is known as post hibernation anorexia, and has been the subject of some intense veterinary research over the past few years. How to deal with it is discussed in the next section. Hopefully you will have followed our previous instructions, and your tortoise will emerge in good condition. As the temperature rises, listen carefully to the hibernating box - you should begin to hear the first sounds of movement.

Rather than follow tradition and wait for your tortoise to emerge from its hibernating box itself, you should remove the box from its winter quarters and warm it up by placing it close to a heater. After an hour or so, remove the tortoise from its box and place it in a warm, bright environment. Repeat the pre-hibernation health checks, then offer the tortoise a drink as soon as it is fully awake. Provided the temperature is correct, this should only take a matter of an hour or two.

Many people experience problems in getting tortoises to drink - in fact almost all tortoises will drink, provided water is offered in a suitable manner. We recommend placing the entire tortoise in a sink or washing-up bowl filled with very slightly warm water up to the level of the tortoise's lower jaw. Simply offering a small dish of water to the tortoise is not likely to stimulate a good drinking response, but actually placing it in water is usually successful.

The importance of *getting the tortoise to drink cannot be overstated. Indeed this is essential, as during hibernation the kidneys accumulate large quantities of dangerous toxins and waste products.* These must be `flushed out' as quickly as possible, or the tortoise may begin to suffer from poisoning. It will certainly feel ill, behave lethargically and remain disinclined to eat.

Drinking is, at this stage, far more important than feeding. Both dehydration and the presence in the body of toxins dictate that every effort must be made to encourage drinking first, feeding later.

The tortoise must also be kept warm as described previously - it is absolutely vital that such temperatures are available in order to speed up activation of the tortoise's digestive system. As the tortoise awakes, certain biological changes take place. One of the most important of these is the release into the bloodstream of a chemical called glycogen, which has been stored in the liver. This provides extra energy to give the tortoise an initial `boost'. Feeding must take place before this is exhausted, or the animal will begin to decline. The glycogen level can be artificially boosted by the daily provision of water with a small amount of glucose in solution (about 2 teaspoons per 250ml dilution), at about 10-20ml per day for an average sized animal. Do not continue this therapy indefinitely however, or dangerously high blood-sugar levels may be attained. All tortoises should very definitely feed within one week of emerging from hibernation. If they do not there is either:

- **A health problem**
- **A husbandry problem.**

In fact, most of our own tortoises feed the same day they wake up, and the rest usually follow within a further 72 hours.

If your tortoise is not feeding by itself within one week of waking up, take the steps described in the next chapter. If this does not produce results within a further three days, do not delay any longer - consult a veterinary surgeon who has particular experience of reptile husbandry, physiology and treatment. Seek the underlying cause of the problem, and do not be satisfied with non-specific `vitamin injection' therapy. There is always a very good reason for a tortoise persistently refusing to eat, and generalised vitamin deficiencies are highly unlikely to be responsible. Good diagnostic techniques, combined with an understanding of reptile metabolism and function, will invariably produce a satisfactory answer. Out of literally thousands of tortoises we have seen over the years with feeding problems, from ancient Galapagos giants to tiny newly hatched babies, we have never yet seen one suffering from anything which a general non-specific `vitamin injection' would correct. It is highly unlikely, to say the least, that yours is the exception. *Whatever you do, please do not delay.* A tortoise which refuses to feed after a week or more of correct temperatures has a problem. It is your responsibility to find out what that problem is and to deal with it effectively.

CHECK LIST

- ❑ **Is your hibernation area protected from frost and yet cool enough for a secure hibernation?**

- ❑ **Is the tortoise completely healthy and a safe weight?**

- ❑ **Are you making regular checks with a reliable thermometer?**

- ❑ **Are the hibernation quarters safe from attack by hungry rodents?**

Terrapene carolina major (Gulf Coast Box turtle).

Wild Testudo hermanni hermanni (Hermann's tortoise) photographed in its Southern French habitat. There are two subspecies of Hermann's tortoise, the Western subspecies (T. h. hermanni) and the Eastern subspecies (T. h. boettgeri). This latter subspecies is the one most frequently kept as a pet.

Testudo ibera (Turkish or Greek Spur-thighed tortoise). Considered by some to be a subspecies of the North African T. graeca, in fact this animal is very different in many ways. It should not be kept alongside North African tortoises as the latter appear to lack resistance to diseases carried by this much hardier, and more prolific species.

Compared to T. ibera (overleaf), North African tortoises are often strikingly marked and specimens from certain localities can attain tremendous sizes. Compare this F. whitei (Algeria) with the nearby Leopard tortoise (G. pardalis babcocki). The taxonomy of North African tortoises is presently much understudied and not all authorities agree on their status and nomenclature. The trade in N. African tortoises has fortunately ended.

Safety is a very important consideration when housing juvenile tortoises. This outdoor terrarium offers protection from predators and a pleasant environment.

Indoor accommodation for terrapins and turtles need not consist of just aquarium tanks; this spacious and naturalistic habitat offers an excellent range of facilities and is a big attraction at Frankfurt Zoo.

Above

A tortoise's shell pattern is good camouflage. Tortoises from precisely the same locality tend to have identical shell patterns (due to localised in-breeding). These were photographed in a field in Tunisia. In their natural environment, even brightly marked tortoises blend into the background extremely well. This serves as protection against predators.

THE SICK TORTOISE OR TURTLE

In all probability, if your tortoise or turtle persistently refuses to eat it is seriously ill. You need expert help - without delay. Do not assume non-specific 'anorexia' - the condition as seen in humans does not occur in tortoises. As a general guide the problem is most often caused by one of the conditions described below. The ability of owners to recognise or eliminate these possibilities is all part of good husbandry, so you should very definitely familiarise yourself with the basic symptoms of these common health problems. All can result in a refusal to feed.

The diagnosis and treatment of a sick tortoise or turtle requires a good deal of logical detective work on the part of both the owner and veterinary surgeon; these animals often do not display very obvious indications of what is wrong, and some familiarity with them is essential if the cause of the problem is to be correctly identified. An initial examination will normally include an investigation of the background to the problem. The answers to routine questions can be extremely useful in this respect:

- Has the turtle only recently been acquired?
- Was it purchased from a pet store?
- Were the conditions there overcrowded or unhygienic?
- Has it recently been mixed with other animals??
- What does its usual diet consist of?
- Is the environment correct for this species?
- Did the symptoms coincide with any other event?

Incorrect feeding and errors of husbandry account for more than three quarters of all sickness reported in captive tortoises and turtles. A careful analysis of the background to the case can very often result in a provisional diagnosis which can then be followed up by clinical investigation.

This also follows a logical pattern:

- The animal is picked up - is it reacting normally?
- Is there a good response to visual stimuli?
- Is limb retraction good? Is the head being held at an unusual angle?
- Is its weight normal?

The patient is then examined visually and in close detail. This can often be very revealing, especially when carried out by an expert familiar with the species in question:

- Are there any unusual swellings or local signs of abnormality?
- Are there any signs of discharge from the nose or tail?

The eyes, ears and limbs are subjected to special scrutiny, the latter are probed along their length in an effort to detect fractures or swollen joints. The shell is then examined carefully all over:

- Is it soft?
- Is it lumpy?
- Are there any evident wounds or other signs of damage or injury?

The plastron is also examined for signs of subcutaneous haemorrhage or bruising and the skin condition is carefully noted. If the external examination results in an `all clear', the examination progresses internally.

The head is extended and the mouth carefully opened. The condition of the mucous membranes is noted - are they a nice, clean healthy pink? If any suspect material is present, a swab is taken for laboratory analysis.

By this point, in perhaps 80% of cases, a few preliminary conclusions will have been reached. Frequently, a satisfactory diagnosis will have been arrived at. In the remaining cases, the full resources of a veterinary testing laboratory may be required. Urine and faeces samples can be examined for parasites, or urea levels analysed. Blood samples can be similarly checked for parasites, elevated white cell counts (which could indicate an infection) and for renal or liver function. If the tortoise or turtle is female, X-rays might be taken to discover if there is an egg problem. Bacterial swabs might be taken from the mucous or from any other suspect discharge for laboratory culture and antibiotic sensitivity testing.

If the correct diagnostic procedures are implemented, sooner or later an answer will normally be forthcoming. Although guess-work may be justified in emergencies, where time is of the essence and every second may count, for the most part *a systematic and logical approach to testudine diagnosis consistently produces the best results.*

Owners can help their veterinary surgeons considerably if they are made aware in advance of the type of questions a vet is likely to ask, and especially if they understand the reasons why such questions have to be asked. Unfortunately tortoises and turtles cannot tell us by themselves what is wrong - but an intelligent and observant owner, working cooperatively with a good veterinary surgeon, can go a long way towards interpreting what is often only a very subtle sign that all is not well.

One of the main ways in which keepers can help is to ensure that they are thoroughly familiar with the habits and captive care requirements of their own turtles. A veterinary surgeon dealing with dozens, or even hundreds of different species, cannot (unless he or she is a specialist) be expected to know the feeding and temperature preferences or typical breeding behaviour of your particular species of Asiatic terrapin for example - but if you do choose to keep such an exotic animal as a pet, there is certainly no excuse for you not to know these things. Books are available, and most Tortoise Societies or Reptile Associations will be only too pleased to offer their practical advice.

The following problems are among those most frequently experienced. Sometimes they occur alone, at other times in combination:

SIGHT DAMAGE

This can be due either to freezing in hibernation or to generalised visual deterioration as a result of extreme old age. **Indications:** lack of response to visual stimuli, refusal to feed, reluctance to walk, collision with objects when walking, moving round in circles. **Treatment:** force feeding or hand-feeding, time and careful nursing. Dehydration is a major danger with any tortoise which will not feed or drink voluntarily. We use Hartmann's solution (an I.V drip fluid based upon sodium lactate). This is given orally at 5% of total bodyweight daily in cases of severe dehydration, reducing as urination begins and the electrolyte balance is restored. High doses of vitamin-A have definitely been shown to assist, particularly in cases of retinal damage and, (to a lesser extent), in cases of cataracts on the lens. This latter can also result from liver or kidney disease, or may again be a simple consequence of extreme old age. Deteriorating eyesight should always be investigated carefully, as it may indicate a more serious metabolic disorder is present.

In our experience most cases of frost-induced eye damage make a good recovery eventually, but in really bad cases this can take several years. Blind or sight damaged tortoises should not be routinely destroyed. Contact one of the tortoise or turtle societies listed in the appendix for further advice and help. Some sanctuaries (including the Tortoise Trust's) can take such tortoises where they can be given the expert care they need.

SWOLLEN EYES

This very common condition can result from local infections, poor dietary management or general debility. In Box turtles the cause is generally one of husbandry, especially a lack of access to wading water and insufficient air humidity. This problem is especially common in aquatic turtles where a poor diet and dirty water are more often than not to blame. However, veterinary diagnosis is essential in all cases. **Treatment:** depends on cause, but often a simple antibiotic eye-ointment brings rapid improvement. Systemic antibiotic therapy (by injection) might be necessary in advanced or otherwise unresponsive cases. Swollen eyes can also be an indication of acute Vitamin-A deficiency, especially in hatchling tortoises and turtles. Swollen eyes are often seen in conjunction with ear abscesses. In such cases they usually disappear after the primary condition has been successfully dealt with. Tortoises or turtles *which cannot see will almost certainly refuse to feed* - such animals may require intensive support therapy including force feeding and rehydration whilst undergoing treatment for their eye problems.

In some cases the eye may be obscured by a thick, yellow film-like substance. There may be a concurrent watery discharge from the eye. This is often seen after an eye injury, or upon emerging from

hibernation. There are two main possibilities: either the inner eye-lid has become infected, or a film of pus is obscuring the lens. A veterinary surgeon will be able to ascertain which. If the latter, it can usually be gently removed. In both cases, treatment with topical antibiotics is called for.

ABSCESSES

Reptile abscesses are usually hard caseous lumps and contain cheesy yellowish pus and other infected matter. They do not normally respond well to purely systemic therapy (treatment by injection) and surgical excision is usually essential in addition. We see many abscesses, the most frequent sites are the ears, the legs, the inside of the mouth and the nares (the nose). Tumours are extremely rare in tortoises, so if you encounter a `growth' in all probability it is an abscess or cyst which can be effectively treated. See below for treatment guide-lines.

ABSCESSES IN THE EAR

The ear is *by far* the most common site for abscesses in tortoises and turtles of all species. When a tortoise refuses to feed, or appears to be generally not well, it is one of the first places which should be checked. **Indications:** swelling in area of ear flap, refusal to feed. **Treatment:** surgical removal by veterinary surgeon. The abscess is opened under a local or general anaesthetic and all of the infected tissue is drained or excised . A careful follow-up programme with frequent re-examinations is essential or a recurrence is highly likely. Even after surgical removal some infected material may remain, and this should be removed as healing progresses; irrigating the area with antibiotic on a daily basis is a useful post surgical technique. If an ear abscess is left untreated, not only is much suffering caused, but eventually death will result as the infection spreads. The same comments apply to abscesses in other locations.

Ear abscesses are *especially common* in American Box turtles. The cause, in this case, is usually keeping them under conditions which are too hot and dry. Terrapins and aquatic turtles can suffer ear abscesses for the same reason - but more often the cause is simply poor water hygiene. All abscesses

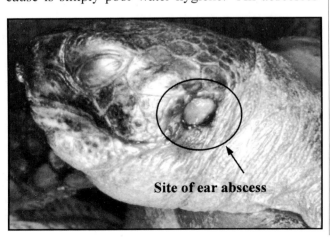
Site of ear abscess

are treated in the same way as those which occur in the ear; very few will respond to systemic antibiotic treatment alone. In almost all cases physical removal and subsequent regular cleaning out and dressing will be required. Betadine® is a useful general antiseptic ideal for application to such infected areas.

SWOLLEN LEG JOINTS

Regularly check the legs (and especially the joints) for signs of unusual swelling or stiffness. They are very prone to abscesses and arthritic-like conditions. Arthritis and arthritis like conditions are relatively common, but they should always be regarded as being very serious. *If left untreated, eventually they will kill.* The soft tissue of the joints becomes eroded and in advanced cases the bones themselves become infected (osteomyelitis). This can be diagnosed by X-rays. **Indications:** the joints are swollen and puffy and the limb may be unusually stiff. The tortoise may limp or not want to walk at all. **Treatment:** in the early stages a course of antibiotic therapy (via injection) is often successful. In very advanced cases, where bone destruction is severe, amputation of the affected limb is often the best and safest option. Tortoises manage very well on three legs, by the way.

It should be noted that one prime cause of such problems is feeding a diet which is too high in protein content; this results in a dramatic increase in generated urea (which is a by-product of the body metabolising the proteins) and this in turn can be deposited in the joints thereby initiating the condition. Herbivorous tortoises which have been fed on cat or dog food, or other very high protein foodstuffs, are most at risk from this rather unpleasant condition which is known as articular gout.

Should a tortoise be encountered which is suffering from this problem, then, in our experience, the most consistently successful treatment programme is to place the animal on an ultra-low protein diet (in order to reduce blood urea levels as quickly as possible) combined with the maximisation of hydration and fluid throughput. Together, this combination will serve to `flush' the excess waste products (including urea) from the patient - the process can however take some considerable time. A period of months, rather than weeks, is typical of the time required for this treatment to take effect. At the beginning of the treatment programme, a biopsy and X-ray are taken of the affected joint. The results of these determine which antibiotic treatment, if any, is most appropriate to the patient. In some cases anti-inflammatory drugs are also used.

SKIN DISEASES

A red, raw and suppurating skin may indicate a severe vitamin-A deficiency. This is most frequently encountered in hatchling and juvenile aquatic turtles where it is usually associated with concurrent swelling of the eyes. If the skin becomes raw and smelly, then a bacterial infection is usually present. Initially this can be treated using frequent Betadine applications, but serious or unresponsive cases will require antibiotic therapy. In such instances, an antibiotic cream or paste often proves very effective. Very severe cases will require simultaneous antibiotic injections - we have found Amikacin, Gentamycin or Framycetin to be most effective as such infections are usually the result of aggressive Gram-negative organisms which are resistant to many common antibiotics.

It is normal for tortoises and turtles to shed some skin during growth phases or due to seasonal factors. Provided the shedding is clean and dry there is nothing to worry about. *If raw or infected patches are present, however, seek veterinary advice without delay.*

BROKEN BONES

These are surprisingly common and usually result from falls. The indications are similar to those outlined immediately above; principally a reluctance to use the limb in question and possibly some localised swelling. Diagnosis is most easily achieved by X-ray. **Treatment:** the leg is usually 'strapped up' in plaster for several months whilst the break heals. Synthetic, non-soluble materials will be required in the case of aquatic turtles. Special care must also be taken with these to make sure that they cannot get into trouble and drown as a result of the temporary loss of use of the limb.

BITES & SCRATCHES

Dogs have often been known to attack tortoises, frequently inflicting some quite horrific injuries. So far we have not seen any evidence of injuries caused to adult tortoises by a cat - although having seen cats in Mediterranean countries enthusiastically hunting for Wall Lizards we don't doubt that very small tortoises, and especially hatchlings, could be in potential danger. In connection with hibernation such injuries are often the result of attack by rats. This is entirely preventable, so take adequate precautions (surround boxes with wire mesh and check regularly). If the worst does happen, clean with a good general purpose antiseptic solution and seek veterinary advice immediately. **Treatment:**

essentially the same as for any wound; a thorough cleansing with Betadine followed by topical (locally applied) antibiotic therapy in severe cases. If rats are the culprits then preventative systemic (by injection) antibiotic therapy might be in order. The same treatment is followed for minor cases of shell damage - but be careful not to confuse a minor injury with the first symptoms of something more serious such as necrotic dermatitis, for example. Keep all sick or wounded tortoises indoors and under cover as fly eggs and maggots can appear with frightening rapidity, especially in the eyes, or around the nose. If discovered in this condition, remove the maggots and wash well immediately with a mild antiseptic or saline solution.

SHELL INJURIES

Damage to the carapace is a quite frequent occurrence; most cases are relatively minor however. One area of shell to inspect frequently is just above the tail - especially if you have more than one tortoise. This area is usually the first to get battered during fights between males or during mating behaviour. If it becomes loose or flaky, keep it very clean and separate the animals for a while.

More serious shell injuries caused by dropping or crushing need *urgent* veterinary attention. We see tortoises regularly which have suffered sometimes quite horrendous carapace injuries as a result of accidents with lawn-mowers and similar garden machinery - this sort of accident could be prevented with a little more care on the part of owners.

If the worst should happen, the severity of the injury will need to be expertly assessed - although it is important not to panic and be too dismayed by something that might look far worse than it actually is. Tortoises can recover from some pretty spectacular damage given good care. Really severe carapace damage can sometimes be repaired using special medical grade plastics and epoxy cements - ordinary fibreglass material is not usually suitable

and should not be used. A few years ago one of our more memorable patients was a little terrapin which was found wandering with a severely cracked shell miles from the nearest water. This was successfully repaired by pinning the shell and cementing everything back into position with a medical epoxy compound. Fortunately, the back legs, although very weak, remained usable indicating that terminal spinal damage had not occurred. The most likely cause of this injury was that the terrapin had been kidnapped from its pond by a heron or similar large bird, struggled free in flight, and fallen to the ground! Fortunately this very lucky little turtle went on to make a complete recovery despite incurring what at first looked like dreadful and quite probably fatal damage.

SERIOUS SHELL INJURIES: practical guide-lines for vets

The following guide-lines are for the repair of severe shell trauma and must not be carried out by anyone other than a qualified veterinary surgeon. The details are included here not as an encouragement to "do-it-yourself" but to illustrate the techniques employed by specialists in this field. The procedures involved are advanced and demand a high level of technical knowledge and experience as well as access to specialist drugs and equipment only available to veterinary surgeons.

These procedures will normally require that the animal is anaesthetised:

- Flush wound with lactated Ringer's solution; follow with topical (dry) antibiotic; suture if coelomic cavity ruptured.
- If muscle tissue is involved, remove tension.
- If a fragmented injury, remove loose pieces in preparation for replacement by inert fibreglass mesh. Plastral injuries where a considerable amount of tension occurs may require drilling and pinning with small steel sutures.

Smaller cracks may only require binding with adhesive tape until natural healing occurs; adhesion of tape to the surface of the shell can be improved by prior swabbing with acetone.

Where a large piece of shell is missing, bridging with fibreglass and epoxy will often be required - however, this is usually best accomplished later on in the healing process rather than immediately. At all times ensure that continued access to or drainage from the wound site remains possible. **There is nothing worse than sealing a wound which still contains an active infection.** With most tortoise and turtle injuries, it is advisable to maintain full access to the wound area until it is evident that all is well. The physical repair to the shell can then be undertaken in safety. A temporary dressing or reinforcement should suffice initially. Only when healing is advanced is a permanent plastic or fibreglass repair made.

These fibreglass-epoxy repairs can be highly successful, but they are by no means easy to accomplish; by far the greatest practical danger is that of `trapping' infection inside the injury. Provided this is avoided, victims of some very major and otherwise probably fatal accidents can be salvaged. A second problem is obtaining good adhesion to the often slightly greasy surface of the shell; a thorough cleansing with acetone immediately prior to application of the epoxy certainly helps here. Large areas of missing carapace can be effectively reinforced with a combination of fibreglass matting and surgical steel wire. The outer coating of plastic should be as smooth as possible to prevent any accumulation of dirt.

Young and rapidly growing turtles pose special problems; generally the best results tend to be obtained with adults whose growth has stabilised. However, we have seen some good repairs made on young tortoises and the attempt is certainly worth making.

SERIOUS INJURIES: First-aid steps for owners

Really major traumatic injuries require expert treatment. **Consult your vet immediately.** If it does not cause any delay, try to telephone (or get someone to telephone for you) the veterinary surgery to inform them of the problem. That way, advance preparations can be made for your arrival. Tortoises and turtles are incredibly resilient creatures and with the proper care can often recover from what at first sight appear quite horrendous injuries - so even when confronted by a tortoise with a leg torn off for example, it is important not to panic. With prompt expert treatment such animals can not only survive but go on to lead a normal life. At least one of our three-legged tortoises regularly fathers hatchlings!

Do not irrigate severe penetrative injuries. There is a danger that you could wash more dirt into the wound than out of it. Leave this stage of the operation to the veterinary surgeon who will irrigate with sterile lactated Ringer's solution in a controlled manner designed not to force any dirt particles deeper into the injury. Ordinary water is not used as not only is it not sterile, but it can remove electrolytes from the tissue - a loss which can be ill-afforded at this time.

Obvious dirt surrounding the wound can however be gently cleaned away using a gauze pad moistened with water. If you have Betadine available soak the pad in a mild solution before use. *Do not apply any ointment or similar substance directly to the injury.*

Apply a gauze pad to the wound to slow the rate of blood loss and to prevent dirt entering the wound. *Dehydration resulting from bleeding can be very dangerous.* In cases of severe bleeding, gentle but firm pressure applied directly to the site of the injury can do much to reduce the flow until expert help can be obtained.

Keep the animal warm and quiet. Shock can be a major contributory factor in cases of serious injury and post-incident trauma should be minimised as far as possible.

Transport the injured animal to a veterinary surgeon as quickly as possible. Topical antibiotics will almost certainly be needed to prevent secondary infection, and following initial stabilisation of the patient, expert consideration given as to the best way to effect a satisfactory long-term repair.

ULCERATIVE SHELL DISEASE

This problem is also known as 'shell rot'. An unpleasant disease usually of bacterial origin, although a mycoses - fungal infection - can also be involved. It is usually encountered secondary to a shell injury or abrasion. **Indications:** fluid, sometimes bloody, 'leaking' from shell. Fluid can often be seen underneath the plates, which may also develop a reddish tinge. **Treatment:** depends upon which bacteria or other organism is involved, and how advanced the tissue destruction is. However, exceptional attention to hygiene is a must. Twice-daily scrubs with undiluted povidone-iodine solution and regular removal of all loose material is essential. In serious cases, daily application of a topical antibiotic agent of known potency against Gram-negative organisms is advisable. Surgery may also be required with the removal of infected necrotic tissue a priority. In our experience 75% of cases respond very well indeed to daily treatment with Betadine alone. *This is, however, a disease which requires expert diagnosis and treatment if the animal is to survive.* Untreated cases invariably prove fatal as the infection degenerates to widespread generalised septicaemia. As with many conditions encountered in captivity, much can be done beforehand in order to prevent the problem:

- With aquatic turtles, ensure water is clean and

well filtered at all times. Change it regularly.

- Avoid exposing the tortoise or turtle to any object which might cut, abrade or otherwise pierce the shell. Burn injuries from inadequately guarded heaters are a major cause of such damage, both in terrestrial vivaria and aquatic turtle tanks.

- If you use a 'natural' flooring material in your vivarium, change it regularly. Artificial substrates should be taken out, washed clean and sterilised on a routine basis before replacement.

- Do not overcrowd animals. This greatly increases the concentrations of pathogens present in the holding area and, in addition, can stimulate aggressive behaviour leading to injuries.

Treat all shell injuries, however minor, with an antiseptic as soon as they occur. Do not allow shells to become caked in dirt.

Shell infections are much more difficult to treat in aquatic turtles than in land tortoises, and are much more likely to spread to other animals. An isolation tank, where sick turtles can be kept entirely separately, is absolutely essential if cross-infection is to be avoided. It is usually best to keep affected aquatic turtles out of water - at least some of the time - especially during the early phases of treatment, otherwise, healing can be extremely slow and medication very difficult to apply with any effect. Overnight is a good time for the application of ointments etc., as the turtle is usually quiet and much less likely to become stressed by its enforced removal

The white area showing on this tortoise's shell is bone, revealed following loss of the outer scutes from a bacterial infection. In time, the bone will dry out and eventually fall off. New tissue will form underneath and healing will be complete. This can take many years.

from water. During the day it can be returned to a separate isolation tank until fully healed. Adopting this simple technique with aquatic turtles can reduce the time taken for the shell to heal by up to 50%.

R.N.S.

`Runny Nose Syndrome' appears to have several causes. **Indications:** may refuse to eat, persistent nasal discharge, tortoise may be lethargic and generally off-colour. **Treatment:** keep all affected tortoises in strict quarantine, as certain forms of the condition are contagious. Also keep the animal warm (not too hot), and maintain good air circulation. Many cases are due to environmental causes - indoor environments and vivaria are often implicated. Antibiotics may be required in persistent cases. Nose-drops are often successful. Recently, a new drug called 'Baytril' (Enrofloxacin) has been used in persistent 'R.N.S.' cases with considerable success. This is delivered by injection every 24 hours over a 20-day period at a dose rate of 5mg to 20mg per Kg. A 'Baytril' nasal flush has also proved useful. This drug has a wide ranging effect against both Gram-negative bacteria and mycoplasma - this latter group of organisms having recently been discovered as causing many previously mysterious respiratory symptoms in tortoises.

Other factors which are often implicated include:

Foreign bodies entering the nares such as grit, dust, grass or food particles. R.N.S. resulting from this is obviously not species selective and can affect any tortoise. Often only one nostril will show evidence of discharge. **Treatment:** flush the nares with sterile water and if necessary antibiotics. Consult your vet.

Hypovitaminosis-A. Where a vitamin-A deficiency exists the delicate tissues of the nose, respiratory tract and eyes are among the first to be affected. Lesions may develop which can in turn become infected by bacteria. **Treatment:** Vitamin-A supplementation with concurrent topical antibiotic therapy if a secondary infection is present. Consult your vet.

RESPIRATORY DISEASE

May be mistaken for an ordinary cold. Rapidly fatal unless treated properly. Indications: mucous and saliva in plentiful evidence, sometimes foaming at the mouth. Obvious difficulty breathing in acute cases. The tortoise will usually hold its head high, and at an unusual angle whilst gaping and gasping for breath. This phase is often followed by collapse, unconsciousness, and eventual death. From first symptoms to death in acute cases can be as little as 4 hours, hence, **at first sign of breathing difficulty obtain expert help without delay.** Beware of terrapins and aquatic turtles which are having evident problems swimming - this can be an early sign of pneumonia. **Treatment:** we have found that an injection of Oxytetracycline can be extremely effective in doses of 50mg/Kg. Ampicillin is also useful, again at 50mg/Kg. Repeat every 48 hours for a course of 5 injections. The new drug 'Baytril' as discussed previously under 'R.N.S.' has also proved highly effective against severe pneumonia. Do *not* routinely deliver antibiotics to tortoises orally. It is virtually impossible to gauge the resultant blood serum level, and it will also have catastrophic effects upon the digestive system. Always treat parenterally (by injection) or topically (by direct application) as appropriate. One useful exception to this is where the recommended treatment involves Amoxycillin which has proved relatively safe in tortoises despite contraindications for use in other small herbivores. Meanwhile keep the tortoise warm and fully hydrated (by stomach tube if it refuses to drink for itself). Prevention is obviously better than cure, so at first sign of `cold-like' symptoms place under close observation. Pneumonia is unfortunately common in all debilitated tortoises, Box turtles, and terrapins. The symptoms of a potential pneumonia should **never** be ignored - seek expert veterinary help at once if you suspect that it may be developing. Pneumonia in a tortoise is definitely a full-scale veterinary *emergency* situation.

MOUTH INFECTIONS

Necrotic Stomatitis is another very serious and unpleasant disease typically of bacterial origin (although cases of viral origin have also been encountered).This condition is almost always fatal without prompt and appropriate treatment. It is sometimes called `mouth-canker' or `mouth rot'. **Indications:** excess saliva production, refusal to eat. Upon opening the mouth a spongy or cheese-like yellowish deposit may be visible. In addition, gums and tongue may have a deep red or purple tinge, possibly speckled with blood. **This disease should be regarded as highly contagious to other tortoises and turtles.** Isolate suspected cases immediately, and enforce strict hygiene precautions. **Treatment:** as much infected matter as possible should be removed gently using cotton buds dipped in mild antiseptic solution. This should be repeated daily. Also the mouth can be gently rinsed with dilute povidone-iodine solution (Betadine). Main treatment consists of the daily application of a topical antibiotic paste or solution. This is continued until the mouth is completely clear of infection, and all lesions have healed. Note that some cases of stomatitis are unusually resistant to certain antibiotics. For this reason, a laboratory analysis and sensitivity test is normally employed to establish the most appropriate antibiotic therapy in any given case. The oral cephalosporins have proved highly effective in some otherwise resistant cases. Tortoises with stomatitis will often need to drink each day, and may also require stomach tube feeding if the treatment is prolonged. Reptiles suffering from stomatitis are at considerable risk of secondary infections, particularly pneumonia, and definitely require expert handling under conditions of exceptional hygiene. Most cases of stomatitis fall into one of several readily recognisable categories:

❑ Simple stomatitis

This condition is typified by a generalised surface accumulation of slimy bacterial plaque which is usually relatively thin and mobile. The organisms found in such cases tend to be unduly resistant to antibiotics and often physical removal of the bacterial build-up combined with regular swabbing with povidone-iodine will clear the condition. As always, however, it is a good idea to take a sample for culture as early as possible - this is invaluable insurance should the infection deteriorate or prove particularly tenacious.

❑ Deep tissue stomatitis

Any stomatitis involving the widespread destruction of tissue, or (in really acute cases) the infection of jaw or palate bones is likely to prove extremely difficult to treat. *Topical povidone-iodine irrigation alone is not adequate in such cases.* A carefully targeted antibiotic programme is essential. This is usually administered both tropically and systemically (by injection). The removal of as much infected tissue as possible under a general anaesthetic may also be called for. The outlook for severe deep tissue stomatitis cases is guarded. Good laboratory work in obtaining accurate antibiotic sensitivity results can however save the day. Recently, several outbreaks of highly contagious deep-tissue stomatitis within tortoise collections have, on analysis, proved to be the result of infection with Herpes-type viruses. Treatment in these cases has relied upon Acyclovir (Zovirax). Results have been mixed with complete cures noted in some cases and 100% fatality in others. The study and treatment of viral disease in tortoises is as yet at a very early stage and much remains to be discovered.

❑ Stomatitis involving the respiratory tract

This is one of the most difficult forms to treat. In such cases the trachea may become physically blocked by accumulated necrotic debris. This will need clearing regularly if the animal is not to choke. An aspirator of the sort used by dental surgeons is useful. Alternatively, judicious work with cotton buds and tweezers can suffice in an emergency. As with deep tissue stomatitis, it is usually essential to combine both locally applied and injected antibiotics. Tortoises with this form of stomatitis may experience severe difficulty in breathing and should *not* be left unattended.

All cases of stomatitis require considerable handling skills on the part of everyone involved in their treatment. Some tortoises (especially large ones) can prove very resistant to what is, after all, often quite a painful treatment regime. It is essential not to distress the animal more than necessary, and not to inflict consequential handling injuries in the process. Be especially careful of causing handling sores at the `grasp points' behind the ears. Whilst some force may be necessary to open the mouth, this must always be well controlled and care must be taken not to damage the beak or the jaw bones. It often helps if two people assist; one to hold the front legs, the other to apply the treatment.

FATAL EPIDEMIC SYNDROME

For some years now tortoise keepers and veterinary surgeons throughout Europe and the U.S.A. have been faced with certain tortoises which present with a series of complex conditions for which no obvious cause can be found and which fail to respond to normally effective treatment programmes. The symptomatic picture of a typical patient can be summarised as follows:

There is often a history of persistent R.N.S./URDS (upper respiratory disease syndrome) or rhinitis. This may degenerate into bacterial pneumonia which is a frequent cause of death. With `ordinary' pneumonia a good antibiotic response is fairly typical - with these animals, that positive response tends not to occur. Or if it does, there is a subsequent relapse and the pneumonia often becomes chronic and unresponsive.

There is frequently a history of persistent gut parasite problems featuring flagellate organisms and in many cases cilliate organisms. Despite treatment with the recommended drugs, these problems may recur on an almost continuous basis. Undigested food is persistently passed, and severe diarrhoea is also common.

There may be concurrent jaundice or anaemia. In some animals there appears to be evidence of acute hepatitis (liver disease). Affected animals may go on to develop a `wasted' appearance with persistent weight loss and appear malnourished despite an adequate dietary intake.

Animals may display symptoms consistent with acute vitamin-A deficiency: poor skin condition, swollen eyes etc. Again, this is observed in animals where the diet is such that under normal conditions no such deficiency should occur.

Finally, death may result from a variety of opportunistic infections and metabolic disturbances; pneumonia, septicaemia, stomatitis and liver failure are the most frequently observed direct causes of mortality. Also seen are mycoses (yeast or fungal infections), mycoplasma induced respiratory diseases and (possibly) secondary infections involving herpes-group viruses.

The exact combination of afflictions varies in individual cases - suggesting that the tortoises are being overwhelmed by commensal ('normal') bacterial organisms as a result of a compromised immune system and generalised debility. In some instances this is most probably associated with a form of viral hepatitis. Specific cases of viral hepatitis have been described in the technical veterinary literature. In other cases it appears that the primary organism may be a mycoplasma. The fact is that the possibility even exists there may be two entirely different types of organism involved; one a virus and one a mycoplasma. At the present time the nature of this disease is not fully understood and research is still in progress. What *is* clear is that there is growing evidence of what appears to be a highly contagious or infectious disease that seems to affect certain groups of tortoises more than others, and for which, at present, no truly effective cure seems in sight. Under these circumstances everyone with responsibility for any captive tortoises or turtles should *exercise extreme caution* when handling new animals, and *especially* when transferring or introducing animals into established collections.

The following guide-lines, if followed, will serve to reduce the spread of any disease and should be adopted as routine in all collections:

- Avoid the random mixing of different species or the direct mixing of tortoises from different geographical origins. Different groups of tortoises may have differing sensitivity or resistance to disease organisms. If possible, each species or sub-species should be maintained separately.

- Adopt rigorous food handling and general hygiene precautions. Wash all feeding utensils carefully and do not feed one group of tortoises immediately after handling another without prior hand washing.

- It is best if tortoises are fed separately. Multiple feeding is potentially an excellent way to spread diseases and parasites. For similar reasons, avoid overcrowding (see later notes also).

- Do not introduce `new' animals into any collection without a prior quarantine period; we would suggest 6 months as a minimum. Note that both viral diseases and diseases caused by mycoplasma can involve 'passive carriers', that is, animals which themselves do not show symptoms but which do carry the disease. *Such individuals may carry the organism in an infectious form for life.*

- Do not take tortoises to meetings where large numbers of tortoises congregate; such meetings are sometimes held by enthusiastic amateur reptile groups, but if viral or mycoplasma pathogens are present, then meetings of this sort would present an ideal opportunity for further cross-infection.

Never, *under any circumstances*, release any captive or ex-captive animal back into the wild. This could have catastrophic consequences for already endangered wild populations. If a tortoise or turtle is sick, then seek qualified veterinary attention as a matter of urgency.

VOMITING

Spontaneous vomiting should always be regarded as a serious symptom. It is frequently caused by:
- Lack of digestive enzyme activity due to too low a temperature
- Parasite infestation ('worms' or flagellates)
- Ingestion of toxic material affecting digestive system
- Generalised septicaemia (blood poisoning)
- Overfeeding or incorrect diet

Vomiting may also occur during force-feeding, or when being handled too roughly. **Treatment:** identify causal factor and treat accordingly. It is important to note that tortoises which are being hand-fed are particularly liable to display symptoms of vomiting. There is often a tendency to overfeed in these circumstances, and rely too much on food items containing excessive protein or sugars (including those found in fruits). Sugar-rich foods, or generalised overfeeding, can result in excessive quantities of stomach gas being generated. This in turn leads to vomiting. A further serious side-effect, due to distension of the gut, may involve respiratory distress - the symptoms of this may easily be mistaken for primary pneumonia. An X-ray, however, will reveal localised tympanitic colic rather than the `shadows' in lung tissue so typical of pneumonia. Tortoises suffering from tympanitic colic often issue loud `gurgling' noises and may demonstrate behaviour consistent with severe discomfort. *This condition should be considered highly dangerous and veterinary assistance should be sought at once.*

SALMONELLOSIS

This disease is most usually associated with aquatic turtles and in fact rarely causes them any serious problems directly; however, it is an important and potentially lethal zoonosis - a disease which can be transmitted from animals to humans and, as such, precautions should always be taken to guard against any possible danger. Provided these steps are routinely adopted when keeping any tortoise or turtle, the risk is low:

- Never clean tanks, cages or filters in the kitchen or anywhere else where you prepare food for people or for other animals.
- Always wash your hands with disinfectant soap after handling any animal. Iodine based soaps (available from chemists) are the most suitable for this purpose.
- Keep all tanks, pens or vivaria scrupulously clean. Use an effective disinfectant regularly. Good hygiene is fundamental not only to preventing any possible risk of human disease, it also greatly decreases the chances of the animals becoming sick.
- Never eat or put anything in your mouth when working with animals.
- Young children, the elderly, or people undergoing medical treatment involving antibiotics, or taking drugs which might affect the immune system, should take special care in the presence of all animals.

These precautions are easy to put into practice, and should become a matter of habit in any good reptile installation.

JAUNDICE

This is often the result of either dehydration or fatty degeneration of the liver due to incorrect diet, however more ominously, jaundice is also a primary symptom of a fatal viral hepatitis which can affect both tortoises and turtles. **Indications:** The tortoise is usually reluctant to feed and may be inclined to hide in corners or bury itself. Mouth inspection may (but not always) reveal a yellowish tinge to mucous membrane and tongue. Undigested food matter may also be passed. **Treatment:** Veterinary diagnosis essential. Keep well hydrated using plenty of water with just a pinch of glucose. Serious cases will require medication, Methionine is especially useful (200mg tablet every 48 hours). A persistently jaundiced tortoise requires specialist veterinary diagnosis and treatment. Laboratory tests based on blood samples can be very useful in establishing an accurate diagnosis.

ANAEMIA

Common in debilitated animals. **Indications:** Pale mucous membranes, weak and listless. **Treatment:** Depends on cause, so veterinary diagnosis essential. However, some cases of pernicious anaemia quickly respond to treatment with Vitamin B12 orally. It should be stressed that an accurate veterinary diagnosis of the cause is vital - **parasite infestations** are one likely factor as are acute renal or hepatic problems.

BURNS

These are surprisingly common, and are usually caused either by a tortoise secreting itself inside a bonfire, or by vivarium inhabitants who have accidents with electrical heaters. Treat as for a normal injury, and seek veterinary assistance.

POISONING

Every summer without fail we receive at least a few sad reports of tortoises or turtles dying as a result of eating toxic garden chemicals. Slug pellets, rat poisons and garden weed-killers are the most frequent culprits. These should **never** be used in any location to which a tortoise might gain access. Most of these chemicals are very nasty indeed and all require highly specific veterinary treatments if the animal is to stand a chance of survival. If you encounter a suspected case of poisoning:
- Seek *immediate* veterinary assistance. All such cases must be treated as *emergencies*.
- Attempt if at all possible to establish the exact nature of the poison; this information can be

vitally important in deciding the best treatment. If a packet or container can be located and taken to the vet with the patient, all the better.

There are a series of standard treatments for many better-known poisons. For example, anticoagulant rat poisons such as Warfarin are usually treated with vitamin-K injections. Most veterinary surgeons will be all too familiar with the effects of these substances as they account for large numbers of `incidental' casualties among domestic pets and wildlife alike.Some common garden plants, such as Daffodils, are certainly highly toxic to tortoises. Plant with caution!

FEEDING DIFFICULTIES

Obvious difficulty with feeding rather than simply a reluctance to feed usually indicates either a mouth infection (see above) or a traumatic jaw injury. We regularly see tortoises and turtles with broken or dislocated jaws; these are all too often the result of mishandling during force-feeding. The point of the jaw is especially fragile, and fractures at this location are common. Dislocated jaws can usually be manipulated back into position, but fractures will require stabilising, sometimes with wire and surgical cement. The healing time in such cases is very long, often running to 6 months or more.

DROWNING

Tortoises and (surprisingly, perhaps) turtles can drown. Land tortoises usually meet this fate by falling into unfenced ponds or streams. Aquatic turtles are more likely to become trapped underwater in a discarded fishing net or other obstacle. Prevention is better than cure in this instance, so securely fence all ponds and make certain that aquaria or pools containing turtles are free of underwater obstructions.

Should you encounter an apparently drowned tortoise or turtle do not give up hope too soon; they may appear dead but still retain a spark of life. Extend the head in a straight line and tip the animal upside down to drain as much fluid as possible from the lungs. Never turn a drowned tortoise onto its back, however, as this may flood any remaining air pockets and hasten death. After draining the lungs, artificial respiration is called for: place the tortoise on its plastron and extend the front legs; then push them in as far as they will go. Repeat this process during transfer to a veterinary surgeon. The vet can deliver an osmotic diuretic and respiratory stimulant. If the animal does recover, pneumonia may follow in the immediate post-trauma period. A short course of broad spectrum antibiotic is therefore a wise precaution.

SORE OR INFECTED TAIL

Indications: manifests as a smelly, unpleasant leak or discharge from the tail. Treatment: irrigation of the cloaca with dilute povidone-iodine solution via catheter. Veterinary diagnosis essential, as one possible contributory factor is flagellate infection : see under **parasites**, below.

DIARRHOEA

Frequently associated with parasite infestation. A sample can be examined by your veterinary surgeon for traces of flagellate cysts or worm ova. The problem is also associated with poor dietary management; too much fruit and insufficient dietary fibre are responsible in upwards of 50% of cases. In aquatic chelonians however, parasites are usually the cause.

PARASITES

Tortoises are particularly prone to two types of worm: long, greyish looking creatures called *Ascarids*,and a smaller, very thin whitish type called *Oxyurids*. Both respond to treatment with a Fenbendazole type wormer called Panacur®, administered orally. Another really excellent (Oxfendazole based) tortoise wormer is called Synathic®. Both Panacur and Synathic should be administered in the form of a liquid suspension in doses of 3ml per Kg body weight. This would be an enormous dose for a mammal, but is perfectly correct for tortoises. *On no account administer ordinary cat or dog worming powders or tablets to tortoises.* These often include chemicals which are toxic to reptiles.

High gut concentrations of worms are often encountered in captive tortoises; there are several reasons for this. Overcrowding is a major factor, as is continual re-ingestion of worm ova from the very restricted living space available compared to that experienced under natural conditions. Worm ova are excreted in the faeces, often in close proximity to the feeding area; under such conditions it is hardly surprising that `worm problems' are commonplace. The best solution is to `worm' tortoises at least twice a year with a high quality ovicidal worm preparation as outlined above - once in the early spring, and again in late summer are good times to undertake routine worming.

Flagellates

Flagellate protozoan organisms are another potential parasite. Flagellate infection often manifests as diarrhoea, sometimes tinged with blood and mucous. It can be serious, and expert veterinary advice should be sought. The recommended course of treatment often involves the use of Metronidazole (Flagyl). An effective dose-rate is l60mg per Kg over 3 days, or a single larger dose of 260mg/Kg, in both cases delivered orally. Keeping tortoises too warm overnight appears to encourage protozoan proliferation as does feeding a diet too rich in protein or sugar (fruits are a major offender in this respect). The main problem is likely to be in re-establishing normal digestion following a very severe flagellate attack. This can be helped by administering natural (live bacteria) yoghurt.

Hexamitiasis is a highly pathogenic infection of the urinary and renal system, symptoms include thickened urine which smells strongly of ammonia. This is invariably very serious, but can be treated with Metronidazole. *Never ignore such a symptom, or irreparable kidney damage may occur.*

SEPTICAEMIA

Generalised septicaemia or blood poisoning can occur as a secondary result of any bacterial infection, but is particularly common in connection with necrotic dermatitis and abscesses. **Indications:** weakness, vomiting, collapse, unconsciousness, sometimes delirium. The plastron may be 'flushed' or pinkish underneath; in terrapins and turtles, the legs or skin may appear unusually pinkish or show small subcutaneous haemorrhages. The tongue may appear spotted or mottled (a useful sign of haemorrhage). **Treatment:** antibiotic required urgently, especially Framycetin or Gentamycin by injection at 10mg per Kg or Ampicillin a 75mg/Kg. Repeat dose at recommended intervals.

SUMMARY

This is not a complete list of tortoise diseases by any means, nor a recommendation for 'D.I.Y.' as far as treatment is concerned. It is merely a guide to what can happen, and what to expect if it does. **The main keys to successful treatment of sick tortoises are prompt recognition, and accurate diagnosis followed by appropriate medication.** Never rely upon guess-work and always seek the underlying cause of any problem. Examinations should be thorough and complete, and where necessary laboratory diagnostic tests should be employed.

Always, without exception, consult a qualified veterinary surgeon and never attempt self-treatment or use antibiotics or other prescription medicines without veterinary supervision. Do not be afraid to seek out a veterinary surgeon with special knowledge and experience of reptile treatment.

Finally, a few general observations.

OVERCROWDING

Generally speaking it is best to keep more than one tortoise. The main exception to this rule is where elderly female tortoises are concerned, these often prefer to be alone or kept alongside another female of similar age. They do not adjust well to being kept in groups containing younger, more boisterous and aggressive tortoises - especially if there happen to be males in the group.

If too many tortoises are kept in too small an area, however, then the disease risk escalates considerably. This is especially relevant to parasitic contagion ('worms' etc.) and to bacterial, mycoplasma or viral infections which positively thrive in overcrowded conditions.

There are a number of organisms in circulation which can have devastating effects and for which little or no treatment is currently available. *The only answer is prevention.* If you accumulate a lot of tortoises, from different backgrounds and origins, then sooner or later you are likely to encounter an infected animal. If this should happen, *all of your existing tortoises* are placed at immediate risk.

The risk is at its worst when different species are mixed together at random. For this reason, we believe that *only compatible species should be allowed to contact each other.* **If tortoises of different kinds are allowed to mate, feed and defecate in close proximity then without a doubt you are simply asking for trouble.**

In fact, in the wild most tortoises only meet other tortoises relatively infrequently. In some areas, for example Greece and Turkey, where population densities are fairly high, meetings occur regularly; in other areas such as North Africa, where densities are by comparison much lower, meetings tend to occur only at mating times when males set out in search of females.

Some tortoises from very isolated habitats do not integrate well with other tortoises at all; especially sensitive in this respect are certain Asiatic species *e.g.* the rarely seen Impressed tortoise (*Manouria impressa*) and the attractively marked Indian Star tortoise (*Geochelone elegans*). These tortoises tend to have a very poor resistance indeed to all 'alien' organisms and should never be mixed with anything

45

other than their own species - for that matter, being rare and endangered creatures they should certainly not even be considered as 'pets' in the first place. Similarly sensitive are many of the North African tortoises which often react quite badly when exposed to more aggressive and `hardy' species such as the Mediterranean spur-thighed tortoise (*Testudo ibera*) or the Hermann's tortoise (*Testudo hermanni*). Not only do they have poor disease resistance but also, being generally less forceful and aggressive in personality, they often fail to compete for food adequately under such circumstances.

American Box turtles on the other hand are extremely gregarious little animals and often congregate in groups even in the wild. Not only do they sometimes gather in groups of 4-5 under a `shared' log, but they also choose multi-occupancy hibernation chambers - some of which may contain as many as a dozen of the turtles over the winter.

STRESS

Stress in reptiles is a problem which should never be underestimated; it lowers disease resistance, affects feeding and in pregnant females can lead to egg retention problems. Most enthusiasts who keep lizards and snakes recognise this factor and take steps to alleviate it. Many tortoise keepers on the other hand are completely unaware of the problem. A little effort directed at reducing stress in captivity can make a great deal of difference to the overall health and welfare of a collection and in our view should be considered every bit as important as good dietary management or environmental control.

ANTIBIOTICS

Avoid extended use of antibiotics where possible. Some antibiotics, such as Lincomycin or Oxytetracycline, can cause considerable digestive upset. Lincomycin is not especially useful, but there are times when Oxytetracycline can be extremely valuable, so apart from reducing the side effects by proper dosing and administration, few alternative options may exist. Some smaller species such as *T. kleinmanni* and *F. nabeulensis* can react very badly to some antibiotics such as Ampicillin and Oxytetracycline as can hatchlings. In such cases, antibiotics must be used with extreme caution, and under conditions of intensive care where any subsequent dehydration or digestive flora `scour' can be immediately controlled. Many bacterial organisms are found in tortoises, one of the most difficult of which to eliminate is *Pseudomonas* and similar Gram-negative organisms (e.g *Citrobacter*

and *Klebsiella*). It is important to identify these where present, and to ensure by laboratory tests that they are sensitive to the antibiotic employed. *Pseudomonas* is found extensively in necrotic stomatitis. Where a definite non-response is noted, resistance may be suspected, so change the antibiotic. New drugs are becoming available all the time, and some, such as 'Baytril' are proving very effective in the treatment of sick tortoises and turtles. Consult a specialist veterinary surgeon for up-to-date advice.

EUTHANASIA

There are obviously occasions when all efforts fail, when an animal's condition indicates that a recovery is no longer possible, or that the degree of suffering likely to be experienced by allowing death to occur naturally is not acceptable. In these circumstances it is usually kinder to put the patient painlessly to sleep in order to minimise distress. This is a decision which must never be undertaken lightly, and should only be contemplated where a terminal outlook, confirmed by expert diagnosis, is already imminent. At the Tortoise Trust, our attitude is that whilst there remains a realistic hope of recovery, the patient must be given every chance. When that hope has gone however, there is little point in prolonging discomfort any longer. The most satisfactory method of euthanasia for chelonians requires an overdose of injectable anaesthetic or proprietary veterinary euthanasia formulation typically based upon barbiturates; such procedures should only be carried out under qualified veterinary direction. This method is entirely painless, quick and reliable. Other methods may not be. Death in tortoises and turtles can be diagnosed using the following criteria:

- Manifestation of rigor mortis
- Tongue colour grey and lifeless
- Physical tissue deterioration
- Centres of eyes sunken and lifeless

Rigor mortis in particular may or may not occur in all cases, it depends upon the physical state immediately prior to death; however, its presence is a good confirmation of death. Where uncertainty exists the best solution is to keep the patient warm for several hours; eventually, one or other of the above indicators will confirm its status beyond any reasonable doubt.

ASSIST FEEDING

With all tortoises and turtles there are times when it may become necessary to resort to either force or hand feeding. This is particularly so in the case of sight damage or where a sick tortoise for some other reason is unable to feed itself. Fortunately tortoises do not find this as distressing as mammals, and from the owners point of view the procedure is both safe and relatively simple. We classify force-feeding in three basic stages: hand-feeding, which is really no more than an encouragement to feed normally; syringe feeding, which is less time-consuming and which allows alternative foods to be employed; and finally, stomach-tube feeding, where semi-liquid food matter is introduced directly into the digestive system by means of a tube passed down the tortoise's throat.

Hand feeding

Ideal in animals which are not in a serious condition, and where encouragement to take food into the mouth is all that is required. It is frequently highly successful with sight-damaged animals. Suitable foods: sliced apple, pears, cucumber and melon etc. **Technique:** simply open the tortoise's mouth, and place the food inside. To open a tortoise's mouth efficiently and safely, simply grasp the animal firmly behind the ear-flaps and jaw with the thumb and second finger of one hand, and firmly press down the lower jaw with the thumb and first finger of the other hand.

Syringe feeding

Obtain a 5 ml or 10 ml syringe from your veterinary surgeon. Alternatively suitable syringes are often sold in pet stores as baby bird feeders. This method can be used in conjunction with the hand-feeding (above). **Suitable foods:** liquidised fruits - prepared baby foods are ideal. To these can be added a vitamin supplement. **Technique:** open the tortoise's mouth manually (as above), and simply syringe small quantities of food onto the tongue to be swallowed naturally.

Stomach-tube feeding

This sounds more drastic and difficult than it actually is. However, care must be taken:

❑   Not to cause physical damage
❑   Not to spread infection

To avoid the former proceed slowly and gently, to avoid the second, be sure to sterilise all implements very thoroughly.

The method is invaluable with very debilitated or sick tortoises who are unable to swallow, or who need food by the quickest possible route. Special diets can be given using this method, and the precise quantity of food taken can be carefully controlled. It is also possible to deliver vitamins, drugs or other substances in exact quantities where required. **Suitable foods:** liquids such as plain water, water containing vitamin preparations and semi-solid items such as plain fruit baby foods, again with added vitamins as required. We are opposed to the use of milk-based high protein food preparations, even in severe cases of undernourishment. We have often noted serious side-effects where these are employed, possibly due to lactose intolerance in some animals, and in other cases we suspect that the high protein input is causing liver and kidney damage. We have, in any case, rehabilitated so many extremely underweight and undernourished tortoises without such materials that we can honestly see no need for them. *Our general policy with all feeding is low protein, high vitamin and mineral content, low fat and high fibre.* This most closely approximates the diet of a wild tortoise. We are becoming increasingly convinced that excessive force feeding on unnatural substances is one reason why so many people experience high rates of mortality in such cases whereas our own experience is that such tortoises usually make a very rapid recovery. **Technique:** obtain a 5 ml or 10 ml syringe, also a dog catheter. Cut to size and fix to end of syringe (length of tube = just over 2/3 the length of the tortoise). Ensure that the end of the tube which is to be passed down the throat is smooth and free of any sharp edges. Lubricate lightly with vegetable oil. Place the tortoise in an almost vertical position, extend neck and head fully in a straight line. Gently and slowly pass the tube down the throat, carefully avoiding the trachea, which is located just behind the tongue. *If resistance is encountered, under no circumstances attempt to force the tube in any way.* Gently and slowly empty the contents of the syringe into the tortoise's stomach.

The amount of food which should be introduced in this fashion has been the subject of some confusion. Our general recommendations are as follows. These figures have been extracted from our case records based upon several hundred animals and we believe them to be highly accurate. Sometimes figures are quoted which are many times in excess of these, but we believe that such over-feeding can prove extremely hazardous, especially to a sick or relatively inactive animal.

FEED QUANTITIES

Remember, these are approximate guide-lines only. If the tortoise has been starved for a long time prior to beginning tube feeding, reduce the quantity initially. Liquids should be provided in addition, preferably by inducing the tortoise to drink voluntarily. In cases of severe dehydration, begin hydrating with fluid at a rate of 4-5% of total bodyweight daily. If oedema (puffiness, or swelling) is noted, and urination is not present, reduce level and seek expert advice; a diuretic may be necessary, as kidney function may be impaired. The most common cause of renal distress is due to solid deposits of uric acid literally blocking the kidneys; a combination of diuretic and oral Hartmann's solution is the most effective therapy, assisted by daily lukewarm baths and physiotherapy of the back legs.

Below: Recommended feeding and hydration levels for tortoises which cannot feed themselves.

Size Range	Feed	Fluid
75-120mm	*2ml X 2 Daily*	*5ml X 2 Daily*
150-180mm	*5ml X 2 Daily*	*8ml X 2 Daily*
220-280mm	*10ml X 2 Daily*	*25ml X 2 Daily*

CHECK LIST

❑ **Remember that an accurate diagnosis is essential if the correct treatment is to be given.**

❑ **Not all veterinary surgeons are familar with diagnosing and treating tortoises: find a vet who is a specialist in reptile medicine or a vet who is prepared to consult those who are.**

❑ **Do not rush into 'force-feeding': sick tortoises are usually more in need of fluids than solid food initially.**

❑ **Be aware that some diseases are highly contagious or infectious. It is vital that adequate hygiene precautions are followed at all times.**

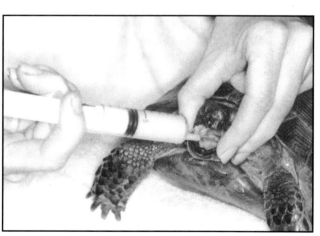

Right

Stomach-tube feeding equipment. A 10ml syringe with a medium sized catheter tibe is suitable for most average sized tortoises.

Left

Syringe feeding a sick tortoise. Note the correct way to grip the head, with the tortoise's mouth held gently open. Use firm pressure, but never force. Keep handling to an absolute minimum to reduce the risk of causing abrasions or pressure sores. Do not overfeed. Use the table (above) for guidance.

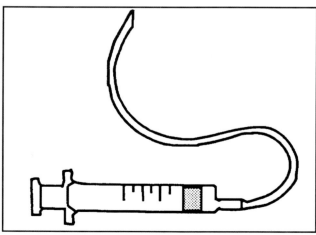

Conservation projects, such as that undertaken for the giant tortoises of the Galapagos Islands, rely upon a wide range of skills on the part of project workers. Dietary and veterinary management is critical, as is a firm understanding of captive breeding techniques. These skills are no less essential in smaller scale projects.....

CAPTIVE BREEDING

At one time, all pet tortoises were taken from the wild. This directly contributed to the decline of these species in their native habitats. Contrary to some reports that populations have recovered now that bulk trade collecting has ceased, we can categorically state on the basis of extensive field experience that this is definitely *not* the case. The damage done was severe and lasting. **Many tortoises face extinction unless effective conservation measures are taken now.** In certain areas of Africa and Southern Europe where once hundreds of tortoises could be seen in a day, it now takes a week to sight a handful.

In such circumstances, it is no longer acceptable to take animals from the wild - the same applies to tortoises from other areas. The only morally acceptable solution for those who wish to keep tortoises in future has to be captive breeding.

At the time of writing, many tropical species are still being collected in the wild. This is without a doubt contributing directly to their continued decline. We do not consider that this is acceptable and we would like nothing better than to see a complete halt to pet trading in all wild-caught animals. Captive breeding offers a way to enhance enjoyment of the hobby of tortoise keeping, it offers a way to learn more (by first hand experience) about the biology and behaviour of turtles and tortoises, and it directly reduces pressure on wild populations.

In short, captive breeding offers a positive way forward - both for humans who like to keep the animals, and for tortoises and turtles who need to be allowed to exist, as they always have done, unmolested in their natural habitat.

There are, however, several important prerequisites which must be met before successful and consistent captive breeding can take place.

COMPATIBLE PAIRS

In all cases it is vital to ensure that potential breeding pairs are correctly matched - it also helps if they are of opposite sexes. This may seem too obvious to even need stating, but you would be amazed at the number of people we encounter who have been trying for ages to captive breed from two females or from two males without realising it.

SPECIES & SUBSPECIES

Another maybe, not so obvious, requirement is that they really do have to belong to the same species and subspecies. Not only are cross-breeding attempts highly unlikely to produce consistently successful results but it is not good practice from an ethical or conservation viewpoint to cross-breed between animals of different genetic backgrounds. For maximum success, make sure that you have a correctly matched pair.

That requirement is, however, not always easy to achieve; it should be remembered that pet trade animals were collected over many years and from very diverse locations. Tortoise populations in the wild tend to have a highly convergent genetic make-up and *little or no genetic material is exchanged with neighbouring populations*. The main reason for this is the lack of mobility demonstrated by most species of land tortoise. Aquatic turtles which live in rivers tend not to possess quite the same degree of genetic `specialisation', although populations residing in isolated lakes may do so. Terrestrial and semi-terrestrial tortoises from physically isolated populations may feature different shell markings, coloration or some other distinguishing feature which sets them apart from even their nearest neighbours. On occasions, these differences may be very profound and in some cases are sufficient to inhibit breeding between individuals from different areas.

The best general advice in these circumstances is to select potential breeding pairs on the basis of close physical similarity; *a pair which is closely matched in the fine details of physical appearance is also likely to share a similar genetic compatibility.*

Although the way in which tortoises mate is fairly standardised, pre-mating behaviour varies quite a lot. Some species , for example, are much more aggressive than others. *Testudo hermanni* males bite the female's legs quite fiercely, whilst *T. graeca* and *T. ibera* males engage in ramming and butting courtship behaviour. Many male tortoises emit a sound whilst mating. This can range from a tiny `squeak' in small species to a full throated roar in giants.

AGGRESSION & COMBAT

Whilst male-female behaviour in tortoises can be

quite energetic, apart from a few relatively minor bites and bruises there is rarely any danger of serious damage being sustained (but see the notes on shell infections in the disease section). This is also generally true of male-male combat in terrestrial species. The situation with regard to aquatic terrapins and turtles is more complex. Here, both courtship and combat between rival males can be particularly violent, and unlike most land tortoises, these species are equipped with extremely sharp beaks designed for predatory use. As a consequence, biting injuries from carnivorous turtles can be severe. It is also the case that many of these species are naturally extremely aggressive; the soft-shell and snapping turtles especially so, although even the smaller species such as musk turtles display a level of aggression quite out of keeping with their size. As a consequence, very great caution should be exercised when introducing any aquatic testudine to another. Nasty injuries are commonplace, and even fatalities are not unknown. It is generally best to make any introductions under close observation, and be ready to separate the animals should serious fighting break out.

AGE OF TORTOISES FOR CAPTIVE BREEDING

It appears from all of the evidence available so far that most tortoises and turtles become sexually active at a certain size rather than at a certain age. This may not be true of all species (e.g. Musk turtles), but it certainly seems to be the case with Leopard tortoises (*G. pardalis*) and most Mediterranean species. In the wild, tortoises tend to grow fairly slowly compared to the rate achieved in captivity and hence mature later. In captivity we know of several cases where 5 or 6 year old males have fathered clutches of fertile eggs. We also have first-hand experience of a 100 year old male becoming a father.

Whilst the age of males is not that critical, very young and very elderly females should definitely not be used in captive breeding attempts. In both cases, the risk of something going seriously wrong is very high, and in our view it is simply not fair to expose them to the danger.

Females can have problems laying eggs. If this happens, the consequence can be a very nasty condition known as egg peritonitis which is often fatal. If a female you suspect is carrying eggs begins to lose the use of her back legs, or appears otherwise unwell, seek veterinary attention at once - without delay. The situation could be very serious indeed. The vet will X-ray the tortoise which will confirm

whether or not eggs are present and if so, how many. Attempts can then be made to induce the female to lay using calcium and oxytocin injections. In really serious cases, it is even technically possible to perform a caesarean section on a tortoise, removing the eggs via a hole cut in the plastron. But be warned: the success rate for this operation is not high. Such problems are usually avoided if a good laying site is available and provided the female is in good condition and is a regular egg layer. Females which have not produced eggs for many years or are obviously elderly must not be subject to captive breeding efforts on pure welfare grounds.

LAYING SITE

It is no use expecting to captive breed tortoises or turtles if you do not provide them with a very high quality environment. *They simply will not be able to lay their eggs properly and may suffer (possibly fatal) egg retention problems as a result.*

Greenhouses make good laying sites for most land tortoises, as do sunny rocky slopes. If the soil is light, but not too sandy, so much the better.

You can very often tell if a female is carrying eggs in three different ways:

- Watch her behaviour closely. She may become unusually active, climbing edges and patrolling perimeters. She might also begin to demonstrate aggression to other tortoises. Sometimes, she may even take on a sex-reversal role and begin to 'mate' on other females.
- In the few weeks before she is due to lay, she may go slightly off her food whilst at the same time steadily gaining weight.
- You can have her X-rayed by your vet. This is really only justified if you begin to get really worried and suspect there may be a problem. There is no evidence, incidentally, that the low dose of radiation received damages the eggs incidentally.

We have noticed that females very rarely lay in the morning; bright, sunny afternoons between 2pm-5pm are usually the times most favoured. If a female simply drops her eggs on the surface, without going to the effort of digging a nest, these eggs are usually (but not always) infertile. Fertile clutches are generally nested properly. It is not known how (or even if) the female can tell the difference.

Clutch sizes do vary considerably, but most species of Mediterranean tortoise on average lay between 6-8 eggs. Large tortoises tend to lay more. Some tropical tortoises lay a very large number of eggs -

Leopard tortoises, for example can lay up to 30.

A good nesting site for Mediterranean species should be slightly higher than the surrounding area, preferably be situated on a sunny, well drained slope and the consistency and texture of the ground should be light and somewhat sandy. If it is too sandy, however, the nesting chamber will keep collapsing and may be abandoned before the eggs are laid. Very dry sandy soil is worst in this respect. Soil which is just very slightly damp (not saturated) and infiltrated with fine plant roots is best and most closely resembles that often chosen in the wild. Well drained south-facing slopes are the sites most consistently preferred by Mediterranean tortoises both in captivity and in the wild.

Turkish Spur-thighed tortoise (Testudo ibera) excavating a nest.

Female tortoises and turtles take a lot of time and trouble in choosing the nesting site as (in the wild) it has to be just right. They are equally fussy in captivity. They spend quite a long time excavating the nest hole with their back legs, and in carefully positioning the eggs as they leave the cloaca, using their feet. Nest digging and laying can take some hours. When it is all over, the female will very carefully fill in the nest hole using her hind legs.

In the wild, her task is over. In captivity, yours has just begun.

TORTOISE & TURTLE EGGS

Tortoise and turtle eggs vary enormously from species to species, in size, weight and texture. Generally. however, the size and weight of eggs remains reasonably consistent within a particular species - although this is not true in all cases (some aquatic turtles demonstrate an amazing range of variation, even within the same clutch). In my earlier book *`Keeping & Breeding Tortoises in Captivity'* (R&A Publishing Ltd.) a table of typical egg sizes from different species of land tortoise is provided, together with data on typical clutch densities and the internal metabolism of the egg.

Tortoise eggs differ from hen's eggs in several important respects: the albumen is chemically quite different, and does not coagulate in the same way; the proportion of shell weight to yolk and albumen weight is very much greater than that of birds; and the eggshell has a crystalline rather than a fibrous structure.

The development of the embryo within the egg is a marvellous example of zoological mechanics - the developing embryo requires calcium to build its skeleton, so extracts this from the calcium-rich egg-shell surrounding it. As it grows, it requires an increasing amount of oxygen and generates an increasing amount of carbon dioxide which must be expired via the egg-shell. Eventually, it has to physically break down the egg-shell in order to hatch. Of course, the constant migration of calcium from the shell contributes greatly to both of these processes - an egg approaching the end of incubation is very much more permeable, and certainly much weaker, than a newly laid or infertile egg.

ARTIFICIAL INCUBATION

Unless you are lucky enough to live within the same bioclimatic range that your tortoise experiences naturally - and few of us are - you will have to incubate the eggs artificially if they are to develop successfully.

As soon as the female has finished laying, carefully remove the eggs from the nest and place them in a plastic container; supermarket margarine and ice-cream tubs are ideal. This should be half-filled with light, loamy earth mixed with fine gravel. Lay the eggs on the surface, do not completely bury them. As described above, most land tortoise eggs are normally hard, whilst semi-terrestrial and aquatic turtle eggs are much softer and more pliable. In general, the latter type of egg needs to be incubated at a much higher level of ambient humidity than the hard-shelled kind.

It is yet another baseless tortoise keeper's myth, by the way, that the eggs have to be removed from the nest in exactly the same position in which they were laid. They don't. Inversion of the eggs will do no harm at all in the first few days, only later on as an embryo is developing is there a real risk of any harm from movement.

There are two basic suitable designs of incubator.

❑ `Dry-type' incubator

This incubator is constructed from 15mm chipboard,

a material with excellent insulating properties. A transparent secondary lid is fitted to allow examination without heat loss; for this, Perspex or similar plastic sheeting rather than glass is suggested. In our incubators a 60W industrial heating element is fixed to the base but a heating pad would be equally suitable. The eggs are placed in plastic cartons as described previously and rest on a lattice-work of wooden bars suspended above the heater. A water tray provides some humidity.

The temperature is controlled by means of an electronic thermostat of the sort used by tropical fish hobbyists. It is extremely accurate and very reliable. We use this design of incubator for all except tropical tortoise eggs, aquatic turtle eggs and Box turtle eggs all of which prefer more humidity.

❑ `Wet-type' incubator

Where a high humidity level is required throughout incubation this type of incubator has many advantages. Because of the humidity levels attained in this system, glass or polycarbonate is the best constructional material and it will generally be found easiest to adapt a suitably sized tropical fish

aquarium to the purpose. The heating element is a 75-100W submersible aquarium-type combined heater-thermostat. Provided that a very high quality unit is employed preferably based upon a magnetic rather than simple bi-metallic switch, high levels of accuracy will be achieved. The author has used a unit manufactured by Visitherm® which is not only constructed to a high standard but also includes a visual indication of temperature. This is cross-checked using a separate hand-held digital thermometer.

This sort of incubator is ideal for Box turtle or terrapin eggs and for most tropical tortoise eggs. It is worth noting that, without doubt, should dehydration occur in eggs which require incubation in a damp environment (as almost all tropical, semi-terrestrial turtle and terrapin eggs do) the embryo will certainly die or suffer serious structural deformity. We incubate most of these eggs in a mixture of damp (not saturated) vermiculite or pearlite and light gravel.

THE DEVELOPING EMBRYO

One problem often ignored by those involved in the captive breeding of testudines is the requirement of

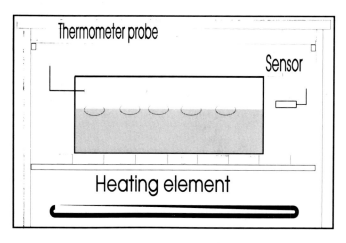

Left

This type of incubator is best suited to hard-shelled tortoise eggs. The outer casing can be made from chipboard or fibre-board. The eggs rest in plastic containers on a wooden shelf above the heating element.

Right

This type of incubator is most suitable for soft-shelled turtle eggs which require high humidity incubation. An aquarium type combined heater-stat provides a sufficiently controlled heat source. CAUTION: make sure the water level is maintained to a safe level!

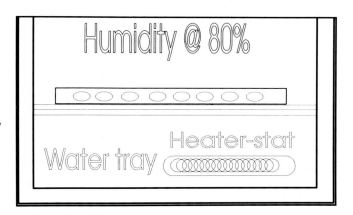

the developing eggs for oxygen. If the eggs are starved of oxygen during incubation then this can result in hatchlings leaving the egg early (the rise in blood CO2 levels acts as the `trigger' for the baby tortoise to hatch). Should this occur, hatchlings will emerge in a weakened state, often bearing unusually large egg-sacs. Incubation in sealed incubators, or in inadequately ventilated containers, can drastically increase both pre-hatching and post-hatching deaths, and it may also contribute to various deformities. The practice of incubating eggs in sealed or almost-sealed containers is therefore not a good idea. On the other hand, the airflow of most bird egg incubators is far too high for the successful incubation of tortoise eggs and can easily lead to over-drying. A purpose-built incubator as described above is definitely preferable. Opening the lid of such an incubator every few days for just a few seconds will allow the air to change and prevent the problems of anoxia outlined above.

INCUBATION PERIOD

The time required for incubation is related to temperature, higher temperatures producing progressively shorter times. At 31°C most *Testudo* species hatch in 8-10 weeks. Very high temperatures, although producing shorter incubation times, can result in severely deformed hatchlings. For maximum success and safety, it is best to keep incubation temperatures within the range 29°-32 °C. Tortoise and turtle eggs, like crocodile eggs, are mostly subject to environmental sex determination (ESD). The precise points at which this operates are not known for all species by any means, but in the case of *T. hermanni* , eggs incubated at or below 29.5°C tend to result in male hatchlings and those incubated at or above 32°C tend to result in females. This is as yet a very imprecise science and much currently remains a mystery. It is now known that ESD does not seem to apply at all to some species - for example, both Wood turtles (*Clemmys insculpta*) and Spiny Soft-shelled turtles *(Apalone [=Trionyx] spinifera)* seem to inherit their sexual identity genetically. Meanwhile, some species reverse the usual 'high temperature = female, low temperature = male rule' adopted by most; Common Snapping turtles (*Chelydra serpentina*), for instance, produce female offspring at both high and low temperatures and males in the middle range.

HATCHING

Hatchlings pierce the eggshell using an egg-tooth, gradually enlarging this opening by biting small pieces from the eggshell and pushing with the front legs.

Hatching can take some considerable time; between 2-5 hours on average. Once access to the open air has been achieved, and the immediate demand for oxygen satisfied, the young tortoise or turtle will often stay in the egg for a day or more, gradually gaining in strength and allowing time for the egg-sac to be properly absorbed. If a hatchling is in obvious

trouble and is clearly weakening then careful assistance can be given.

Do not ever initiate hatching artificially - even if it appears that the 'normal' incubation period is long past and hatching is overdue. Chelonians have been hatching without assistance from humans for millions of years and really don't need our unwelcome (and usually untimely) interference. *If you find yourself having to break open eggs to get live hatchlings then look again at your incubation technique.* You are going badly wrong somewhere.

Hatchling care

Despite their really minute size (most measure around 30mm long) the actual requirements of hatchling tortoises and turtles are no different from those of adults. Young tortoises and turtles are entirely independent and surprisingly alert - some even start feeding before they have left their eggshell. Sometimes the hatchling still retains its yolk-sac which sustained it through the incubation period. This can be quite large and is attached umbilical fashion to the underside, thus preventing mobility. These hatchlings are best left quietly in the incubator for 24 hours or so whilst the yolk-sac is gradually absorbed.

Their diet is basically the same as for adults (although they have a somewhat higher than normal calcium requirement), and environmentally, they need exactly the same range of temperatures and humidity as adults of the same species. In the case of

Box turtles and many aquatic species, juveniles are much more carnivorous than adults - as maturity is reached the diet changes to include more vegetable matter.

Safety

All juvenile tortoises and turtles are very fragile physically so need to be housed under very safe and secure conditions. We normally use one of our smaller adult vivaria, divided up if necessary into several sections. Temperate species can go outside in good weather, but again a very high level of physical protection is essential - birds will eat hatchling tortoises, for example. Rodents such as rats are another potential menace. Protect all juveniles in a totally escape-proof (and entry-proof) area which is completely covered with solid wire mesh.

Do not mix adults and small juveniles in the same environment - nasty accidents can happen, especially during feeding. This is especially critical with carnivorous or semi-carnivorous species. *It is highly dangerous to mix hatchlings and adults for a number of reasons and the wise keeper will maintain them completely separately.*

Other than taking such precautions, we treat hatchlings exactly the same as we treat adults. Juveniles can also be hibernated (provided, of course, that they belong to a species which hibernates naturally in the wild of course). Simply take all the care you would when hibernating any very small tortoise.

The main thing to bear in mind is that if you do get the diet wrong, or fail to maintain the correct environment even for a short time, hatchlings and small juveniles will deteriorate *very* much more rapidly than a fully grown adult. With suitable care, however, there is no reason why one day, your hatchlings should not be proud parents themselves.

CAPTIVE BREEDING QUESTIONS & ANSWERS

Captive breeding generally, and especially the incubation and handling of tortoise and turtle eggs, are subjects which give rise to many questions on the part of beginners. Some of the questions we are asked time and again are summarised below. These particular points seem to cause much confusion, so are worth highlighting here even though the general principles of captive breeding have already been outlined above.

Can I `candle' eggs periodically (by shining a light through them) during incubation to check if they are viable?

Yes, you can. But we do not recommend that you should. It involves unnecessary additional handling and does not actually make any difference to the final outcome. Rather than subjecting eggs to such examinations, we recommend patience.

At what point should I assume eggs are infertile and discard them?

This is always a difficult decision. Our own practice is simply to wait until it is obvious - one way or another - that the eggs are bad. Such eggs either remain transparent, the yolk settles to the bottom, or they explode! Even if incubated at relatively high temperatures, we would not expect to be sure for maybe 7-10 weeks. If in doubt, leave the eggs alone.

If eggs are late in hatching at what stage should I crack them open to help any hatchlings out?

Our view is that this sort of intervention is rarely successful and is more often than not a prelude to disaster - how can you be sure that the eggs really are `late'? If hatchlings are so weak that they are unable to leave the egg unaided then something is already going drastically wrong somewhere. We would look to a genetic incompatibility or poor incubation technique. Anoxia, or oxygen starvation, is one possibility. Prevention is infinitely better than the `cure' in this instance.

Can female tortoises have eggs even in the absence of contact with a male?

The short answer is yes, they can, but are in fact less likely to.

Is there a safe maximum age for breeding females?

Not exactly, but if a female has not had eggs for many years we would be very wary about subjecting her to breeding attempts. There is a high incidence of (fatal) egg-binding in such cases. It is much safer, and considerably more successful, to employ only healthy young females in captive breeding exercises. These very rarely experience any problems and fertility rates are also likely to be much higher.

Are eggs left lying on the surface, rather than nested properly, ever fertile?

Just occasionally. More often than not they are infertile. If no attempt at all was made to nest them properly, it is probable that the female was merely discarding them.

Sometimes the eggs produced by my female tortoises have a rough texture, almost like the surface of a golf-ball. What does this indicate?

Such eggs have usually been retained for a much longer time than is normal - or safe. Investigate nest-site availability. This sort of egg usually has a much thicker than usual shell, and in our experience is never fertile. Such eggs are often implicated in egg-binding and can prove very difficult to lay.

My terrapin always lays her eggs in the water, and although I incubate them they never seem to hatch. What is going wrong?

In the wild, terrapins and turtles leave the water to nest. They also do so in captivity, provided that a suitable site is made available. Terrapins and turtles are very selective about nest sites, and if your terrarium does not provide an appropriate site will often discard the eggs in the water where they rapidly become saturated and damaged. The answer is to provide a sufficiently large and accessible artificial nesting site. This should be warm and damp. A spot-light overhead often
helps. I have found that many turtles prefer to nest in soil which is infiltrated by plant roots - so planting the area might also help. The presence of a few leaves also provides some degree of privacy and cover, again this can help to make the turtle feel secure during the vulnerable nesting phase. The substrate depth required will vary according to the size of animal. Smaller specimens such as European Pond turtles (*Emys orbicularis*) typically dig nests up to 10cm deep, larger species such as Painted turtles (*Chrysemys picta*) may excavate nests twice that depth. Most prefer a loamy, sandy soil as nesting substrate.

Do all the eggs from a single clutch

hatch at about the same time, or are some later than others in leaving the egg?

There can certainly be a considerable delay between emergence of the first hatchling and the last - in the case of Mediterranean tortoises we have experienced periods of up to 18 days and even longer may be possible. With some tropical species the time scale can be very extended indeed. This effect is noted even in highly accurate and stable incubators, and only seems to happen occasionally.

Is it safe to allow tortoises or turtles of different species to mate and produce hybrid offspring?

This is not so much a question of safety, but rather of wisdom and advisability. It is very undesirable to produce hybrid offspring from any non-domesticated animal. There is always the possibility that the resulting genes could find their way back to the wild. In general, hybridising tortoises and turtles is not easy. *If you are hoping to captive breed chelonians, then the most successful formula by far is to employ only closely matched and carefully selected true pairs.* We do not feel that the deliberate generation of hybrids can in any sense be justified.

Hatchlings are very active, and sometimes fall onto their backs. How long can they survive in that position?

It very much depends upon the prevailing environmental conditions; directly under a basking lamp, for example, *fatal overheating could occur in a matter of minutes.* Direct exposure to strong sunlight could produce the same result. In a moderate or mild environment there would be no immediate danger. The same thing of course also applies to adults. The main problem facing the overturned tortoise is that of overheating and inability to thermoregulate. It is definitely inadvisable to leave hatchlings unattended in the presence of high temperature sources - a moderate background heat source at such times is much safer in this respect.

Is it wise to allow hatchlings and juveniles to hibernate? Some books suggest that they should be kept active indoors for at least the

first 5 years.

In the wild, hatchlings live alongside adults. They are therefore subject to exactly the same environmental and climatic conditions. All tortoises - both adults and juveniles - respond identically to these conditions. When the conditions are such that adults hibernate, so do the juveniles. In fact, throughout most of the Mediterranean, eggs are laid in May-June, hatching occurs in September, and by November the hatchlings are experiencing their first hibernation! They emerge again in spring at the same time as the adults (usually in March). Therefore, it is biologically perfectly normal for even very young juveniles to hibernate. That said, it is important to take very special care as the room for error in respect of temperature is slight (the smaller body mass of a juvenile means that the core temperature responds more quickly to ambient fluctuations than an adult under comparable conditions). You can indeed overwinter hatchlings - but it is definitely not necessary to do so, nor should they be maintained in this way indefinitely. A carefully controlled, short hibernation is quite safe and is definitely recommended, if not for the first year, then certainly from the second. Deprivation of hibernation can disrupt the natural cycle, and lead to dangerously accelerated growth.

The topic of captive breeding and hatchling care is covered in considerable depth in this author's "Keeping & Breeding Tortoises in Captivity" (R&A Publishing, 1990) and also in the 50 minute video "Incubating Eggs & Rearing Hatchlings" (Carapace Videos, 1993). This video is available by mail order from the Tortoise Trust in all world television formats and covers such topics as incubator construction, housing and feeding.

INDEX

FURTHER INFORMATION

The following organisations can supply a range of information, advice and help to tortoise and turtle keepers. Most publish regular newsletters which contain news on captive breeding, conservation, veterinary matters and book reviews.

THE TORTOISE TRUST*
BM Tortoise
London
WC1N 3XX
England (Tel: 0267)-211578

NEW YORK TORTOISE & TURTLE SOCIETY
163 Amsterdam Avenue
Suite 465
New York
NY10023
USA

CALIFORNIA TURTLE & TORTOISE CLUB
P.O. Box 7300
Van Nuys
CA 91409-7300
USA

SAN DIEGO TURTLE & TORTOISE SOCIETY
P.O. Box 519
Imperial Beach
CA 91933-0519
USA

NATIONAL TORTOISE & TURTLE SOCIETY
P.O. Box 66935
Phoenix
AZ 85082-6935
USA

SOPTOM
Village des Tortues
B.P. 24
3590 Gonfaron
France

The Tortoise Trust will, on receipt of an SAE or International Reply Coupon send a complete list of books, videos and other information relating to the care and conservation of tortoises.